# How To Get Your Book Published

## Inside Secrets of a Successful Author

---

## Robert W. Bly

**What readers are saying about...**
## How To Get Your Book Published

> "This book is destined to become another great classical work equal to Dan Poynter's *The Self-Publishing Manual*."
> *-Jerry Buchanan, editor, Info Marketing Report Newsletter*

Can Bob Bly really help you find your niche, write a proposal, sell your book idea to a major New York publisher, and become a published author? Here's what readers of *How To Get Your Book Published* say....

"Thanks for your tips...I contacted a publisher — and signed my first book contract 2 weeks ago! I'm currently in contact with another publisher on 2 other books ... thanks!"
—*Wendy Swope, Victor, Idaho*

"*How To Get Your Book Published* contains a lot of valuable information, especially for the novice. I learned a lot. I especially liked the presentation of the pros and cons for self publishing, acquiring and benefits of using an agent, and the specific procedure to follow to publish a manuscript."
—*Louise Froehlich, Mt. Arlington, NJ*

"*How To Get Your Book Published* is a clear, concise and straight to the point manual on how to get a book published. It gives enough information to help someone start organizing their material and write a professional proposal."
– *Barnaby Kalan, Toronto, Ontario*

"I liked the entire book. Everything in *How To Get Your Book Published* was either explained or resources for obtaining the information were given. I would recommend the book to others."
—*Leonard Henderson, Chicago, IL*

"Fantastic! I am getting concrete results, and getting them rather quickly. Thanks for showing me the way."
—*Rick Belloff*

"As I result of the information you provided, I wrote a successful proposal and got my first book published...which is selling quite well at bookstores and on amazon.com. Thanks again for your superb insights and for giving me the courage and the knowledge to quit my job and write full-time."
–*Michael Sincere*

"Inventive ideas which I found very useful."
—*Jim Crosby, Tallahasse, FL*

"Found your advice right on target.
—*W. Terry Whalin, Colorado Springs, CO, author of 40+ books*

"Thanks to you, I'll be making more money this year. I hate to gush, but you really are my idol."
—*Joanna Slan*

"I absolutely love your book. I have searched for a great reference book on writing and feel I've finally found one I can understand in plain English."
—*Jennifer B.*

"You address the nitty-gritty of writing in an interesting manner. The personal insights you share are very helpful."
—*Sara Shapiro*

"I find your common-sense approach both refreshing and highly informative."
—*Dennis Gilbert, Dexter, MI*

I've just finished your book and I'm so grateful to have it as a resource as I begin the process of writing a book and getting it published. Your book is fantastic!
—*Alison Burns*

"I have received valuable information from several of Mr. Bly's books."
—*Judith A. Henry, Tampa, FL*

"Thanks for all the tips, tricks, and sheer inspiration."
—*Debora Egan, Calbary, Alberta, Canada*

"It is so nice of you as an established writer to help struggling writers get a foothold in this industry. Thank you so much!"
—*Steven R. Dixon, St. Peters, MO*

"I've read several others but yours is very practical and straightforward. Thanks for putting together an outstanding book."
– *Tom Coens*

"Just wanted to mention that I got my first assignment after only one query. I also received a second. I do appreciate the sharing of your success with those of us who like to write and want to make a living at it."
—*Richard Y. Colley*

Library of Congress Cataloging -in-Publication Data
Robert W. Bly

How To Get Your Book Published – Inside Secrets of A Successful
Author Second Edition
ISBN 0-934968-14-4

1. Reference: Writing and publishing   2. Authors and publishers

Quantity discounts are available for business, educational or sales pro-
motional use. For information, please contact: Special Sales Department,
Roblin Press, 405 Tarrytown Road PMB 414, White Plains, NY 10607
Telephone: (914) 347-5934   Fax: (914) 592-1167

# DEDICATION

To Bob Kalian —
friend, teacher, and colleague

# ACKNOWLEDGMENTS

Thanks to the thousands of writers who have read my books and articles, taken my seminars, listened to my tapes, and shared their experiences with me. Researching the answers to your questions, concerns, problems, and challenges gave me the inspiration — and motivation — to write this book.

Thanks also to the many editors and publishers who have bought my books. Writing these books and book proposals, negotiating and reviewing the contracts, and making these sales gave me the expertise and knowledge to advise others on how to do the same.

# CONTENTS

# INTRODUCTION

Have you ever asked yourself one or more of the following questions? If so, this book can help make one of your dreams come true — the dream of writing a nonfiction book and getting it published.

*"I have led a fascinating life and have a great story to tell. Or, I know someone who has led a fascinating life, and I want to tell that person's story. I know it would make a great book. Why do I keep getting rejection letters from the big New York publishing houses?"*

*"I'm an expert in my field and have valuable knowledge other people can benefit from. No one else has covered this information in book form before. How do I find the right publisher, make them understand the need for this information, and get them to pay me an advance and publish my book?"*

*"There are already so many books on my topic in the bookstore. How can I convince publishers to do one more — mine — on the same subject?"*

*"As a writer, I dream of someday holding a printed book with my name on the cover as the author. But it seems as if everyone — writers and nonwriters alike — wants to write a book and get it published. Realistically, what are my chances, and what can I do to tip the odds in my favor?"*

On the following pages you will find the results of my experiences over the past 18 years in getting my books published. The specific tips and techniques I include are not theory…they are based entirely on what has worked for me and for other authors. Here's what can happen when you follow my instructions:

➤ You come up with an idea for a book you want to write.
➤ You propose the book to a major New York publishing house.

➤ A publisher agrees to publish your book. They pay you an advance of $5,000 or $10,000 or even $25,000 or more ... before you've written even a single word of your book. Sound too good to be true? It happens every day.

➤ You write the book, hand it in, and then wait. Anywhere from 3 to 9 months later, you receive copies of your finished book in the mail. You hold it in your hands, admire it, and enjoy the deep satisfaction that comes from having published a book.

➤ Your book is reviewed in magazines and newspapers. Radio and TV shows have you on as a guest. Your home town paper does a big feature article on you. All your friends and neighbors see it. Readers call you up to thank you for the book, praise your work, and ask you to speak before their groups, clubs, and associations. Magazines ask for permission to run chapters of the book as articles ... and they pay you for the privilege of doing so.

➤ The book sells thousands of copies. The publisher keeps it in print year after year. You begin to get royalty checks every 6 months paying you for all those books being sold ... thousands of dollars in extra income every year. And your editor at the publishing house begins asking when she can take a look at your next book idea. Heaven on earth!

Sound like an impossible dream? It's a dream, all right, but a very possible one. I know because I've done it. Dozens of times. Thousands of other people have done it, too — many who don't write nearly as well as you do, don't have as good a story to tell, or don't have information as unique and valuable as yours. If we can do it, you can too.

All you have to do is come up with an idea. The rest of what you need to become a published book author is in this book. In fact, I'll even show you how to come up with lots of good book ideas, if you don't already have one.

This book is written for anyone who wants to write a book and get it published. I envision you as falling into one of the following categories:

➤ People with a story to tell, a message to convey, information to communicate, or knowledge to share. You have something to say, and a book seems a natural forum in which to say it. But you don't know what to do next. Or you think you know, but you aren't getting the results you expected. *How To Get Your Book Published* shows you step by step how to transform your idea and desire to write into a published book. Your book can become a reality ... sooner than you think.

You do not have to be a professional writer to write a book and get it published. According to prolific author Herman Holtz, the majority of nonfiction books are written by nonwriters who are specialists in the subject matter of their books. These folks include managers, engineers, accountants, lawyers, technicians, programmers, chemists, home makers, small business owners, gunsmiths, locksmiths, radio disk jockeys, cooks, cops, and workers of several dozen  other classes and categories. "Most probably will not write more than one or possibly two books in their entire careers," says Holtz, "but writing even one book is a major achievement in which one can take great pride."

➤ Professional writers and would-be writers. Many people start not with the message, idea, information, story, or knowledge, but simply with the burning desire to write a book and get it published. *How To Get Your Book Published* explains how to come up with marketable nonfiction book ideas that publishers will buy — and how to sell your book idea and get a publisher to give you a contract for a four or five-figure advance.

➤ Other professionals in all fields. Professionals in virtually every field of study and human endeavor — from attorneys and landscapers, to psychotherapists and personal trainers, to entrepreneurs and software engineers — know something other people want to know and would pay for in book form.

Aside from pride and personal satisfaction, to professionals, the benefits of publishing a book are numerous. For academics, publication can help secure tenure. For other professionals, being a published author can result in more business, greater income, increased prestige, and invitations to do workshops and seminars at handsome fees. It looks good on a resume and can help open doors for you when you are looking for a new job or seeking a promotion. Getting published is a criteria for some professional certifications like the CMP (Certified Meeting Professional.)

One thing you should know up front: *How To Get Your Book Published* is short on theory and long on practical step-by-step instructions and how-to advice. In it, you will find the specifics of how to write a book and sell it to a big-time publisher. You'll also find advice on selling your book to smaller, more specialized publishers or even self-publishing it, if you desire. Everything you need to know to get your book published is covered in detail.

You may be wondering how qualified I am to guide you. Since 1982, I have had 45 nonfiction books published with 10 more currently under contract. My advances have ranged from $2,000 to $35,000. Like many of my readers, I am not a full-time book author (most of my income comes from freelance writing done for corporations). I tell you this not to brag ... but simply to assure you that when I discuss how to write and sell nonfiction books to the big publishing houses, I know what I'm talking about.

I do have one favor to ask. When your book comes out, can you send me a copy of the publisher's press release or catalog, so I can know first-hand of your success? You will be more excited than anyone when your book is published. But when you tell me *How To Get Your Book Published* helped make it happen, I too will be thrilled. You can reach me at:
Bob Bly
22. E. Quackenbush Avenue
Dumont, NJ 07628
phone (201) 385-1220
fax (201) 385-1138
e-mail: Rwbly@bly.com

# CHAPTER 1

# SO YOU WANT TO WRITE A BOOK

Let me share with you an opinion based on personal experience: Few events in a writer's life are as thrilling as the day your first book is published.

Imagine that you've completed your manuscript, had it accepted by the publisher, and publication is scheduled for this month. Your editor has promised you an advance copy, and you've been eagerly checking the mail each day.

Finally, it arrives. You tear open the envelope, and hold in your hands a beautifully printed, 200-page hardcover or paperback book. It takes your breath away: The colorful cover shows the title and the author's name. And the author is —*you!*

Soon, the book shows up in bookstores and the library. The local newspapers call to interview you. You are featured as a guest on radio shows ... perhaps even on cable or network TV. Book reviewers write glowing reviews, published in your favorite magazines. Royalty checks from the publisher begin to pour in, and the publisher asks, with eagerness and enthusiasm, "When will you be sending us your next book?"

Sound impossible? Not at all. In fact, by following a series of eight simple (but essential) steps, you can sell your nonfiction book idea to a major publishing house, get a $5,000 to $25,000 advance, and become a published author.

### You can write a book — and get it published

Now, I don't know you personally. But I am going to make some assumptions about you.

The first assumption is that you like to write. If not, then I assume you have some valuable information, or an important message or fascinating story you want to share with the rest of the world.

The second assumption is that you have one or more ideas you think would make a good book, or that you know yourself capable of coming up with such ideas.

I believe that everyone has at least one good book inside them. But if that's true, why is making the transition from unpublished writer to published author such an "impossible" task for so many people? Why do so many writers live in quiet frustration, never to express themselves in print or experience the joy of holding a book with their name on it?

The reason is lack of knowledge concerning the publishing process and, more specifically, the process of marketing and selling your book idea to a major New York publishing house.

And that's where this book can help. You already have the intelligence, the talent, and the creativity to write a nonfiction book. *How To Get Your Book Published* shows you how to put your book idea into marketable form and sell it to a major New York publishing house.

Step by step, you learn exactly what you have to do to come up with a winning book idea, create a selling proposal for it, find an agent (or sell it yourself), get a publisher to make an offer, negotiate the deal, sign the contract, collect a four or five-figure advance, and get your book published.

This "inside information" has been jealously guarded by the small group of published book authors who know the process but don't want to share their knowledge, for fear of the competition you will give them.

But as one of those published authors, I am breaking with the ranks, sharing the secrets, and telling you exactly what it takes — and what you have to do — to sell your book and get it published.

Why? Because, as a "how-to" author and seminar leader, my mission in life is to improve the lives of others by teaching them what I know. Writing nonfiction books — and getting them published — is something I know well. Now I want to share the information with you.

### THE FOCUS OF THIS BOOK IS ON "MAINSTREAM" PUBLISHING

This book is not about vanity publishing or self publishing although we will look at these subjects in later chapters. It is about selling ideas and getting book contracts from major publishers such as HarperCollins, Doubleday, Macmillan, Random House, and other large book publishers.

When you follow the steps in this book, here's what happens: Instead of you paying to have your book printed (as with self-publishing or vanity presses), you get an advance of $5,000 to $25,000 or more from a "real" publisher whose books you'll find on the shelves of Barnes & Noble, Borders Books, Brentanos, and other bookstores nationwide.

Your publisher pays to have the book edited, typeset, printed, bound, and distributed to the bookstores. The publisher also will do the marketing, and publicizing of your book. You just write and then sit back and collect the royalties —anywhere from 60 cents to $3 or more per copy sold (chapter 9 tells you exactly what kind of royalty to expect).

## LEARN FROM MY YEARS OF EXPERIENCE

Since I started writing in 1982, I have published more than 45 nonfiction books with numerous major NY publishers including McGraw-Hill, Prentice Hall, New American Library, Consumer Reports Books, Henry Holt & Company, John Wiley & Sons, HarperCollins, Macmillan, and many others. More than ten additional books I've written are soon to be published by these and other firms. You can check my credentials by looking in *Books In Print* or *Contemporary Authors*, both available at your local library.

Many of these books have been solid sellers. A few did better; a few did worse. One sold only 4,000 copies; another sold 47,000 copies in one year; a third is now in its fifth printing with more than 60,000 copies sold. I have had foreign editions printed in Spain, Japan, and England, and sales to numerous book clubs including Fortune and Writer's Digest. My advances have ranged from $2,000 to $35,000.

Some nice things have happened as a result of the books. I have been featured in numerous publications, including *Nation's Business* and *Entrepreneur*, and have been a guest on over a dozen radio programs. Publishing books has led to numerous invitations to be the featured speaker at meetings and corporate training sessions, at fees ranging from $1,000 for an hour speech to $4,000 for an all-day seminar.

Readers have also hired me to consult with them and their corporations for fees of $1,000 to $1,600 per day, with several long-term relationships resulting. After my first book was published, I was invited to teach a course in writing at New York University, which I did for several years. To promote my most recent book, I appeared on television (CNBC).

For me, the greatest reward is when a reader writes or calls and says, "I read your book; your information worked; and you changed my life — thank you." I treasure my collection of testimonial letters from readers, now in the hundreds. I save every one I get. You should, too.

'I tell you all this not to brag, but to assure you that my techniques work. I personally have successfully applied the approach detailed in *How To Get Your Book Published* to sell over 45 books in 17 years — a rate of approximately 3 books per year (and writing books is not my full-time job).

Now, I am certainly not the richest, most successful, or most prolific nonfiction book author around. Far from it. But with 45 books sold, I do know what it takes to write a successful nonfiction book and sell it to a big-name publisher. And I have written *How To Get Your Book Published* to help you do the same.

My writing income today is in six-figures, and many nonfiction authors are earning more than I am. Julie Strasser, for example, got a $200,000 advance for her first book, a profile of the Nike corporation. Says Strasser: "The only difference between somebody who has written a book and somebody who hasn't written a book is that they've done it, and you haven't done it — yet. They are not smarter than you."

### THE NONFICTION BOOK MARKET IS BOOMING

As discussed, *How To Get Your Book Published* deals with traditional or "mainstream" publishing — that is, getting your nonfiction book published by a conventional publishing house — as opposed to self-publishing (paying a printer or vanity press to have your book printed). Although the last two chapters deal with the self-publishing option and point you to some very useful resources in that area, my focus is traditional publishing, not self-publishing.

The techniques described here were developed for, and have been thoroughly tested in, the selling of nonfiction books. I have never written or published a novel (my one work of fiction is a children's book published by Banbury/Dell, *Ronald's Dumb Com-*

*puter*, and I sold one short story to *Galaxy* magazine), so my knowledge of selling fiction is extremely limited. Writer's Digest Books (phone 513-531-2690) has published a number of useful books on writing and selling short stories and novels. If you want to write fiction, call them for a free book catalog. They also have good books on writing nonfiction.

When deciding what type of book you want to write, consider the rewards — and the greater potential market — of writing nonfiction vs. fiction. Nonfiction can still be "literary." And your chances of making a book sale are far greater with a solid nonfiction book proposal than a novel.

As John Naisbitt pointed out in *Megatrends*, today we live in the Age of Information. And in this information-oriented society, the demand for informational and how-to books is on the rise. For example, according to *Publisher's Weekly,* of the 50,000 books published each year, approximately 90 percent are nonfiction. Instructional nonfiction is always in demand; *Books in Print* lists more than 2,250 titles beginning with the words "how-to."

In a recent survey, the Book Industry Study Group found that one of the two top reasons people read books is to gain knowledge (the other is for pleasure). According to *Insight* magazine, "A recent Gallup survey found that nonfiction has soared in popularity in recent years."

*Hoover's Guide to the Book Business* reports that book sales of the U.S. book publishing industry in 1992 were $17.1 billion. Of this total, 27 percent was for trade books (hardcovers and trade paperbacks of nonfiction and fiction books sold primarily in bookstores); 26 percent was for textbooks; and 17 percent was for technical, scientific, and professional books. In 1994, Americans bought more than 1 billion books — a 31 percent increase in sales since 1991. According to *Publisher's Weekly*, worldwide book sales exceeded $80 billion in 1995. And the market continues to expand. The Association of American Publishers reported that U.S. book sales totaled a whopping $23 billion in 1998.

A cover story in *Freelance Writer's Report* newsletter says, "Looking for hot topics to research or target your next book? As the population ages, book sales are expected to be greatest in the following fields: reference, history, religion, biography, investment, instruction." So the market for nonfiction is big. And growing.

## WHY WRITE A BOOK?

You have some desire to write and publish a nonfiction book. Otherwise, you would not be reading this book.

Writing a book and having it published can be fun, exciting, and rewarding. But, before you go forward, think about why you want to write the book. What rewards are you seeking? Some of your expectations are probably on the mark; others may conflict with reality.

Here are some of the reasons why people write and publish nonfiction books, along with the results you can realistically expect to achieve:

### MONEY

*When asked by Esquire magazine what he would have done if it hadn't been for writing, novelist Richard Ford replied, "Make more money."*

Although best-selling authors can make millions from their book sales, only a small minority — less than one book in a hundred — of the books published become best-sellers. Earnings for most book authors are much more modest. Jerome Judson, a writer specializing in "literary" nonfiction, says his average book sells only 8,000 copies. And a book can easily take him one or two years to complete.

Chapter 9 will give you a clear picture of how much money you can realistically expect to make from your nonfiction book. As you will discover, it is not a fortune.

Many first-time nonfiction authors earn an advance of $5,000 to $10,000, which is not a lot of money, considering it can take you 3 to 9 months or more to write the book. Of course, if the book sells well you will receive additional royalties over the years.

The most recent survey from the American Society of Journalists and Authors shows the average author earns only $20,000 to $25,000 a year from writing!

Certainly there are exceptions. *Dianetics*, the self-help book by science fiction author L. Ron Hubbard, has sold more than 17 million copies, according to the Hubbard Dianetics Foundation. If the author's royalty rate is 50 cents a copy, the book has earned $8.5 million in royalty payments — not bad for a single project.

The bottom line: You can make extra money from book writing. But the chances of it making you rich ... or even earning you a living ... are small. As we'll discuss later, many book authors use the books to generate ancillary income from related activities such as speaking, lecturing, consulting, and training.

This can bring in some nice additional profits. For instance, after my book, *Business-to-Business Direct Marketing* was published, a marketing director at a major computer company read it and invited me in to do seminars, consulting, and copywriting. My bill to them over the next few years exceeded $70,000 — more than ten times the advance the publisher paid me for the book.

## FAME

Most nonfiction authors do not achieve fame with the general public such as a rock and roll artist or movie star does. Instead, you become well known to a smaller but perhaps more appreciative audience: the readers of your book, which can number in the thousands. If you write multiple books within a given field, you will gain a measure of fame within that field.

A single best-seller does not, ironically, insure fame: Many authors whose books have been on the best-seller list are forgotten, and their books put out of print.

Is writing books a glamorous profession? "Only if your idea of glamour is staring at your computer screen for long stretches at a time each day," writes Diane Cole in an article in *The Writer* (March, 1996).

## PRESTIGE

The fact that you have written a book and had it published adds permanent prestige to your resume which will last for life. Your being a published author impresses others. Your reputation — both as a writer and an expert in the subject matter of your book — will grow. Having a book published is a credit you'll always include in your biography.

Since people view authors as experts, writing a book will make you an expert on your topic in the eyes of the public.

I recently heard the definition of an expert as "someone who doesn't have more information than other people, but just has it better organized." If that's true, then writing a book really will make you more of an expert, since it forces you to think and write about your topic in a clear, logical, easy to follow fashion. When I write a book on a particular topic, I always learn a lot about that topic — and how to make it accessible to others — during the research, organizing, and writing process. I'm sure you will too.

Edward Uhlan, author of *The Rogue of Publishers Row*, notes that just because a person has written a book, the general public thinks he or she is an authority on the subject matter. You can see proof of this on Oprah and the other talk shows. Whenever the producers do a show on a particular topic (e.g., "Men Who Hate Broccoli and the Women Who Force Them to Eat It"), there are usually five guests — two people who are the victims (in this case, men forced to eat broccoli), two people who are the villains (in this case, women forcing the men to eat broccoli), and, inevitably, one person who has written a book on the topic (in this case, the author of *Broccoli and Relationships*).

The late science writer Isaac Asimov, who wrote more than 475 books, tells how during a radio interview, he was unable to answer some of the interviewer's questions about the human brain. The radio interviewer was puzzled at Asimov's inability, and asked, "Didn't you just write a book on the human brain?" Asimov replied, "Yes, but I have written hundreds of books on dozens of subjects, so I can't be an expert in all of them. And I am not an expert in the human brain. But, there is one thing I am an expert in."

"What's that?" the frustrated interviewer asked.

"I'm an expert on being an expert!" replied Asimov. "Do you want me to talk about that?" The interviewer declined to take Asimov up on his offer.

### SATISFACTION

While some people don't enjoy writing their books, almost every author enjoys seeing the finished book published and basking in the glow of "being an author." Writers in particular view authorship of a book as an important career milestone, and may feel unfulfilled until the goal is realized. "There are a great many writers who have never published a book and burn to do so," observes author Herman Holtz. Selling your book, writing it, and having it published will satisfy that burning need within you, if you have it.

## PROFESSIONAL DEVELOPMENT

Becoming an author will benefit you in your career or business ventures. The credential of having a book published makes you more interesting to potential employers, while in academia, the book fulfills the "publish or perish" requirement for tenure and promotion. If you are a businessperson or professional, and you write a book on your field of expertise, it will bring you many new clients and help you close sales you might not otherwise have made.

The Atkins Center, a clinic in New York City, for example, probably gets many patients who call as a result of having read one of Dr. Atkins's books, including *Dr. Atkins's Health Revolution* or *Dr. Atkins's New Diet Revolution* (they have 10,000 patients). One TV commentator told me he was hired, without previous TV experience, because a producer had read his book on real estate. Books generate opportunities like this for as long as they remain in print ... sometimes even afterwards.

## COMMUNICATION

Why do so many people want to be writers, speakers, or teachers? The urge to communicate what we know with others is one of the strongest human desires. "Many people have accumulated experience, ideas, and know-how that others can use," writes Herman Holtz. "A book is the way open to all of us to put it to good use and prevent it from perishing needlessly." By writing a book, you take what you have learned and pass it on to others for their amusement or education. It's a nice way to help and entertain others while expressing yourself and your ideas.

## COMPULSION

"I always knew I would be a writer," says Jean Lowery Nixon, author of more than 100 books for children, in an interview with *SmartKid* magazine. "When I was 10, I sent a poem to a children's magazine and it was printed with my name. It went to my head and I've never been the same since."

Many of us are compelled to write books. Novelist James Brady calls the desire to write books "an addiction those of us afflicted by it are powerless to resist." Poet Jarold Ramsey says, "I write in order to make things more real — familiar, forlorn, and taken-for-granted things, including the people we carry along with us."

Writing books can indeed become an addiction, so be warned. Fortunately, it's an addiction that does you no harm and brings you and your reader pleasure, wisdom, and knowledge. So by all means, if you are compelled to write, indulge yourself.

## FUN

Whether you have fun writing and marketing your book depends on who you are. Many nonwriters consider writing a tedious mental chore to be avoided at any cost. Even many writers dislike writing. They like being a writer but find the work itself difficult.

Fortunately for me, I love to write. If you do too, you'll enjoy writing a book. It's a meaty project that gives you a lot of flexibility and freedom to express your thoughts.

Each project has its own pleasures. When I wrote my massive, 800-page *Advertising Manager's Handbook* for Prentice Hall, it was hard work, but intellectually stimulating. More recently, another publisher called and ask me to write a short quiz book on the TV show, Frasier, starring Kelsey Grammer. Basically, I just watched the show, jotted down interesting points of trivia, and typed them up as questions and answers. It was easy, pleasant work, and this makes me one of the few people I know of who has actually gotten paid for watching TV!

If you don't particularly like to write, writing the book may not be fun. One alternative is to use a ghostwriter (see chapter 10 and appendix K). You'll have fun talking about your subject when the writer interviews you. The writer will do the hard grunt work of transforming transcriptions of your conversations into a book. Another alternative is to write the book with a coauthor who does half the work. The two of you motivate each other and make book writing a less lonely occupation. More than half a dozen of my 45 published books have been written with coauthors.

## POSTERITY

"Few of us are able to leave monuments of stone and metal, but the immortality of a book bearing your words is a monument to which you can aspire," says Holtz. "With a book, you can leave a sign of your passing, something of your persona, and, most important, a few words that may warm and inform your family, your friends, and strangers."

# CHAPTER 2

# EIGHT KEY STEPS TO BECOMING A PUBLISHED BOOK AUTHOR: AN OVERVIEW

This chapter presents my proven formula for writing and selling nonfiction books to major New York publishing houses.

Is there one single method for writing and selling nonfiction, one magic formula? No. Each author has a slightly different approach. You will use what works for you. That may be my formula, a variation of it, another author's approach, your own approach, or a combination of these.

What follows is a tested 8-step method that has been proven to work for me and other authors who have tried it. It's one way to sell a nonfiction book to a publisher ... and I know for a fact it works. The proof? I have gone through this process personally 50 times, and sold 47 books as a result.

### ADVANTAGES OF THE 8-STEP METHOD

There are four advantages to following the guidelines in this book:

FIRST, it saves you an enormous amount of time and effort. In my selling method, you sell the book to the publisher first, on the strength of a well-crafted proposal, then write it only after you have a signed contract and advance payment in hand. Doesn't that make good business sense for the author?

Many authors write the entire book first, then go out and try to find a publisher. A mistake, in my opinion, for two reasons: First, it requires an enormous investment of time and work in an idea that may never sell. And second, for nonfiction, most publishers actually prefer to see a proposal rather than a completed manuscript — because it saves reading time — so handing in a completed book may actually reduce your chances for a sale!

SECOND, my method is proven to work. I use it on every project and, as I've said, have sold dozens of books to publishing houses over the past 14 years. All of my proposals follow the same formula. If you want to learn how to do something, find someone who is doing it successfully, study their method, and model your own efforts after it. You'll get the results you want.

THIRD, my success rate is very high. Of the book ideas I have taken to "full proposal," I have sold approximately 90 percent of them. Only two or three did not sell, and I predict that eventually I will be able to sell one or two of those, based on current interest from publishers.

FOURTH, my method is logical, simple, and easy-to-follow. "You break everything into a series of easy steps," said an attendee at one of my book publishing seminars recently. "That makes the whole process far less intimidating."

To many of us, the idea of writing a book may indeed seem a bit daunting. You will have an easier time if you stop focusing on "writing a book" and instead focus on the immediate step in front of you — whether it's researching your topic, generating ideas, creating the book's table of contents, or even writing up your bio. These smaller tasks seem less intimidating, more doable, and each one completed brings you one step closer to your ultimate goal.

By the way, this concept of breaking a large task into small, manageable steps is useful in virtually every type of writing. When I am writing a book, I break it up into chapters, then further divide each chapter into subtopics. This way, instead of facing the daunting task of writing one big 200-page book, I simply have to write 100 two-page mini-essays on the 100 subtopics in my chapter outline. That's easy!

### THE 8-STEP METHOD AT A GLANCE

Each of these steps is so important, I've devoted a separate chapter to it. These are chapters 3 through 10 that follow.

But it helps to have a concise overview of the process before you start. Here, then, are the 8 steps to *How To Get Your Book Published*:

### STEP 1: COME UP WITH A GOOD IDEA FOR YOUR BOOK

If you already have a good idea, move on to step 2. If not, see chapter 3 for ten techniques guaranteed to help you think of many ideas for books you can write.

Some first-time authors are intimidated by this step. They feel they lack the creativity to come up with good ideas.

My experience is that all of us are capable of coming up with good ideas, including ideas for books. The hard work is not coming up with the idea; it's writing the book.

Isaac Asimov, the prolific science and science fiction author, said that he would frequently get calls from readers who had ideas for science fiction stories. Their proposal to him was that they would supply the idea, he would write the story, and they would split the profits 50-50.

"I have a better idea," Asimov always told these callers. "I'll give you an idea for a story, you write it, and when it's published, you send me 50 percent of the profit."

No one ever took him up on his offer.

### STEP 2: EVALUATE YOUR BOOK IDEA

There are many ideas and titles that sound good, but once evaluated with a critical eye, must be rejected because they are not commercially viable and would not appeal to a publisher.

To determine whether they think an idea has potential, editors employed by large publishing houses ask five critical questions about the proposed book. In chapter 4, you will learn what those questions are ... and how to use them as a tool in evaluating your ideas on your own before you present them to a publisher.

When I ask potential authors why they think a publisher would want to publisher their book ... and why a reader would want to buy and read it ... a lot of them answer, "Because it's a good book" or "The subject is important."

In today's marketplace, that's not enough. Remember: According to the survey cited in chapter one, people read either for information or entertainment. Your book has to entertain or inform them. A book that does neither is going to be extremely difficult to sell.

## STEP 3: CREATE THE CONTENT OUTLINE

Once you decide on a topic for your book, I recommend that you develop a content outline. As shown in chapter 5, a content outline is similar to the table of contents you find in any nonfiction book in the library or bookstore, except it's more detailed and fleshed out. I'll show you how to write a content outline, and provide examples you can follow in developing your own outline.

Developing the content outline has several purposes. First, it helps you determine whether you can produce enough text on the subject to fill a book. Second, it is perhaps the single most powerful tool for convincing publishers that your book idea has merit. Third, it will save you an enormous amount of time when you sit down to write your book proposal and the book itself.

I always make my content outlines detailed rather than sketchy. I am convinced this is important in selling the book to a publisher. Chapter 5 presents actual content outlines from a number of book proposals I did, all of which were bought by major publishing houses.

## STEP 4: WRITE YOUR BOOK PROPOSAL

The successful book proposal has eight sections, each containing very specific information. In chapter 6, you'll see what these sections are and how to write them.

The book proposal is often the most mysterious part of the book publishing process, especially to beginners. The reason: You know what books look like, because you've seen hundreds of them. But chances are, you don't know what a book proposal looks or sounds like, because you have never seen one.

In chapter 6, instructions for writing the various sections of the book proposal are accompanied by examples from real-life book proposals that were successful in the marketplace — that is, they generated an offer from a major publishing house. In addition, a complete book proposal is shown in appendix D, so you can see such a document in its entirety. You don't have to use my style of proposal; publisher's do not have a "standard" for proposal writing to which you must adhere. But why not model your own proposals after the sample presented in chapter 6? After all, the sample proposal sold the book, and the format works!

## STEP 5: GET AN AGENT

Although it's possible to sell directly to the publishers, I recommend you get a literary agent. In chapter 7, you'll learn where to find agents, how to get them interested in representing you, how much the agent gets paid, and how to work with your agent successfully. Also discussed: Book ideas you are better off selling on your own.

## STEP 6: SEND YOUR PROPOSAL TO PUBLISHERS AND GET AN OFFER

If you have an agent, chapter 8 will show you how the agent sells your book to publishers, and what you can do to help. If you choose to go without an agent, I'll give you tips for approaching publishers directly, including several special strategies you won't find elsewhere. We'll cover tactics for approaching major New York publishing houses as well as smaller and specialized publishing firms.

## STEP 7: NEGOTIATE YOUR CONTRACT

If you have an agent, the agent negotiates the contract on

your behalf, with your input and approval; if you don't have an agent, you handle the negotiations yourself. Either way, you need to know about such things as advances, royalties, first and second serial rights, termination, copyright, gross vs. net sales, and other key contract points. Chapter 9 explains them in detail, and shows you what to ask for vs. what you can expect to get.

### STEP 8: WRITE AND DELIVER THE MANUSCRIPT

Chapter 10 gives specific procedures that make it easier to write your book and deliver your manuscript on time.

In most instances, these 8 steps are done one at a time, in sequence, not simultaneously. Feel free to follow closely the samples and examples in the text, while adding your own unique touch or "spin." Don't be afraid to copycat or model your own efforts on what has worked for others; this is often the quickest route to success.

### WHAT ABOUT CHILDREN'S BOOKS?

Does this 8-step procedure apply to children's nonfiction books?

If you are writing a children's book that is primarily text — such as a longer work of nonfiction, or nonfiction aimed at older (ages 10 and up) children — the answer is "yes." Follow the same steps outlined in this chapter, and the same book proposal format outlined in chapter 6.

For picture books, you can submit the full manuscript. This would be the text only — there is no need to illustrate the book until a publisher has contracted for it. But if you are an illustrator, have teamed up with an illustrator, or feel it's critical for the editor to see the type and style of illustration, you can submit one or two sample illustrations along with the manuscript.

Your picture book manuscript should be accompanied by a one-page cover letter. The cover letter should sum up the idea of the book, explain why your book is different from other published books on the same topic, and summarize your credentials, both as an expert in the subject matter, if you are, and any previous writing credits. If you don't have credentials, attach a bibliography showing the extensive research you've done on the subject. If you have discovered any new or unusual facts or findings on the topic, say so in your letter.

"An increasing emphasis is being placed on developing brand-name lines and series," writes publishing consultant James Forbes in *The Insider's Guide to Book Editors, Publishers, and Literary Agents* (Rocklin, CA: Prima Publishing). "If divisions and imprints with specialties in the arena of young readers seem to be closing off the traditional avenues used by rookie talent to get to them, it's due to circumstances that have much to do with corporate consolidation at the larger houses, as well as insider advantages of personal contacts at smaller start-up operations."

There is room for both the original children's book as well as packaged book series. The rising popularity of packaged series may actually be in your favor. Books that are part of a successful series usually have higher sales than they would if published as a stand-alone title. And publishers need writers to create more books for ongoing series.

### WHAT YOU WILL FIND IN THE REST OF THIS BOOK

The core of *How To Get Your Book Published* is the 8-step method detailed in chapters 3 through 10. But the book contains some additional material you may find useful.

Once your book is published, you want to sell lots of copies. Chapter 11 shows you how to effectively promote and publicize your book — on your own as well as working with your publisher's publicity department.

*How To Get Your Book Published* assumes you want to get published by a major publishing house. But this may not be the case. Chapter 12 compares traditional or "mainstream" publishing another popular publishing option — self-publishing — and includes a list of resources including "print-on-demand" to consult if you decide to self publish.

In chapter 13 we will look at the newest publishing options

including 'paperless publishing' that the Internet has opened.

In addition, there are a number of useful appendices. Appendix A provides a list of some of the top publishing firms. Appendix B provides an equivalent listing for literary agents. Both appendices show you where to go to obtain additional names not on my lists.

Appendix C is a standard "permissions form." As I discuss in chapter 10, when you want to reprint lengthy material from other works in your book, you need to get the copyright owner's permission. This is the form you use.

Appendix D is a sample book proposal. Study it carefully. Feel free to copy my format when doing your own proposal.

The book proposal in Appendix D sold, and Appendix E shows the contract from the publisher who bought the book. Note my annotated comments concerning the various terms and clauses.

When your book is published, your publisher will write and send out a press release for it. Appendix F shows the press release for *How To Get Your Book Published* as written and distributed by the publisher, Roblin Press.

You can help the publisher promote your book by providing them with the information they ask for in their author's questionnaire. Take the time to complete it. Be specific and detailed. Appendix G shows a sample author's questionnaire that is fairly typical. So you can start gathering some of the required information now.

Finally, Appendix H lists publications of interest to book writers, Appendix I lists organizations for writers, Appendix J is a helpful glossary of book publishing terms, and Appendix K lists ghostwriters, "book doctors," freelance editors, and other professionals who can help you prepare your manuscript and present it to publishers.

If you need anything else, feel free to call me for advice. My phone number is 201-385-1220. I'll be happy to answer any quick questions over the phone, without charge. If you need more in-depth professional help on a paid basis, I'll probably recommend that you call one of the folks listed in Appendix K. When you do, please tell them I sent you. Thanks.

# CHAPTER 3

# COMING UP WITH A GOOD IDEA FOR YOUR BOOK

Many people who buy *How To Get Your Book Published* or attend my book publishing seminars already have a book idea in mind, and want help getting it published. "Every nonfiction book writer carries dozens of half-formed book ideas in his head at once," says John Gunther. "You need only let them mature at their own pace." If that's the case with you, skip this chapter on generating book ideas and go directly to Chapter 4, "Evaluating Your Book Idea."

Other readers and seminar attendees, however, are in a different situation. They may have a strong urge or desire to write a book, but are stuck on coming up with a suitable topic. If you fall into this category, here are 10 sources of ideas for books you may want to write:

## 1. JOB EXPERIENCE

An obvious but often overlooked source of book ideas is your job. Thousands of excellent books have been written by authors about a skill, expertise, or career experience gained on the job.

This is how I came to write my first book, *Technical Writing: Structure, Standards, And Style* (McGraw-Hill). My first job after graduating college was as a technical writer for Westinghouse Electric Corporation in Baltimore.

After several months writing technical materials, I began to feel the need for a writing guide to assist technical writers with matters of style, usage, punctuation, and grammar (for example, does one write "1/4" or "0.25" or "one-fourth" in technical documents?). Being book-minded, I went to the bookstores and found nothing appropriate.

My idea was to do a style guide for technical writers modeled after the best-selling general writing style guide, *The Elements Of Style*, by Strunk and White. I wrote a content outline and book proposal, and began to pursue agents and publishers.

In my case, I was extremely lucky: The first agent who saw *Technical Writing* agreed to represent the book, and within 3 weeks, he sold it to the first publisher to look at it, McGraw-Hill. The advance was $8,500 — not bad for a first-time author in 1981 for a short (100-page) book.

Not every book since has sold so quickly and easily. But subsequently, I have written a number of books based on skills and experiences gained in various careers and jobs.

Do you hold a highly desirable position or do you work in a glamorous industry? Then you can write a book telling others how to get into your line of work.

Have you developed specific and valuable skills such as computer skills, selling, marketing, finance, negotiating, or programming — skills that others need to master? There's a need for a book telling them how to do it.

## 2. Teach A Course

There are many opportunities for you to design and teach courses to other people: at work, at adult education evening classes at the local high school, community colleges, association meetings, and even university level.

If you get the opportunity to teach a course, keep in mind that the topic and content outline you develop for the course may have appeal to a publisher as the outline for a potential book on the same subject.

Example: In 1981, a private seminar company offering low-cost public seminars in New York City asked me to do an evening program in marketing and promotion for small business. The pay was lousy, but I accepted. A year or so later, I took the course title and outline, turned it into a book proposal, and sold my second book, *How To Promote Your Own Business,* to New American Library, a large Manhattan publishing house.

If you want to write nonfiction books, there are two advantages to teaching a class or seminar. First, in developing and teaching the course, you will simultaneously be doing most of the legwork necessary to produce a book on the subject. Therefore, once you've given the course, transforming it into a book is a relatively quick and easy next step (or at least quicker and easier than doing a book from scratch).

Second, teaching the course positions you as an expert in the subject, making you more attractive to book publishers. They figure that anyone who can give a course on the topic must have a substantial amount of information and expertise to share. If you taught the course at a prestigious, well-known institution, that further boosts your credibility.

## 3. Taking Courses

Taking courses can also give you a fresh infusion of ideas and information that can become the basis for a book.

Example: The same private seminar company I was teaching small business promotion seminars for offered a number of courses in different career areas which, as an instructor, I could take for free.

After taking several programs, I came up with the idea of doing a career book on how to break into some of the more exciting, glamorous industries and professions, such as music, film, advertising, travel, and television. The book, *Creative Careers: Real Jobs In Glamour Fields*, was published by John Wiley & Sons, another large New York publishing house.

Warning: When you take the course, don't steal or plagiarize the instructor's seminar, reprinting it word for word as your book. Just consider it a starting point, and supplement it with additional research from many other sources (seminars, books, articles, interviews, etc.).

If the instructor does have good information you want to reprint (e.g., lists of contacts and resources), get his permission in writing. You can also ask the instructor if he or she will agree to be interviewed by you for inclusion in the book.

## 4. WRITE ABOUT YOUR LIFE EXPERIENCES

"It is in the totality of experience reckoned with, filed, and forgotten, that each man is truly different for all others in the world," writes Ray Bradbury in *Zen In the Art Of Writing*.

Every person, every life, is unique, and this is why I say that everyone has at least one book inside them: What has happened to you has not happened to other people, and your experiences will make for a book that is either instructive, entertaining, moving or any combination of these.

This applies to everyone. For example, if you have chosen to remain single, you can write *Living Alone And Loving It* or a similar book on the joys of being single. If you are married with children, you have unique experiences as a parent, and can share your knowledge and experiences with others in an entertaining or informative book. If you are married but have been unable to have children, you have credibility to write a book on infertility. If you and your spouse have not had children by choice, you can write a book on *Choosing To Live Child-Free*. If you have only one child, you can write *Raising The Single Child*. If you are a single parent, you can write *Straight Talk And Advice For Single Parents*.

Another example: In 1982, the New York City engineering firm employing me told me I would have to relocate to its manufacturing headquarters in Wichita, Kansas. My fiancee did not want to leave Manhattan, so I resigned and started a new career as a self-employed industrial writer, producing brochures and data sheets for chemical companies and industrial equipment manufacturers.

The transition from employee to freelancer was an educational experience, one I knew many others would go through (or would hope to, some day). This became the topic of my book, *Out On Your Own: From Corporate To Self-employment,* published by John Wiley & Sons.

## 5. Write About a Process or Task You Know How To Do

Through work, leisure, or life experience, we all have done things that many other people have not done, and therefore know a good deal more about these things than they do. The inexperienced would like to learn from your experiences and avoid your mistakes, and a book is the ideal vehicle for this.

For instance, after resigning from the engineering firm and becoming a self-employed industrial writer in 1982, I was forced to learn how to succeed in the commercial writing field on my own; there was no book to guide me. I made many expensive mistakes, and learned from experience.

To help other writers speed the learning curve and avoid these expensive mistakes, I wrote *Secrets Of A Freelance Writer,* published by Henry Holt & Company, a New York City publishing house. The book is about the process of running a freelance writing business, covering everything from getting started and finding clients, to setting fees and negotiating contracts.

## 6. Write About Your Hobby

Hobbies that fascinate you no doubt fascinate a lot of other people. As a hobbyist, you have much more knowledge than a journalist or other outsider who would have to research the field from scratch. Why not turn your hobby into a profit-center by writing a book about it?

One of my hobbies is collecting comic books. I love Superman, Batman, Wolverine, and the other DC and Marvel superheroes.

When I graduated college in 1979, I burned with the desire to write a book and get it published. I pursued two book projects.

One was a Harlequin romance novel. I started this not because I enjoy Harlequin romance novels — I've never even read one — but because they published a guidebook on how to become a Harlequin author, and I figured it would be easy to do.

I was wrong. I wrote 40 pages of the worst Harlequin romance novel of all time (all I remember about the manuscript is frequent reference to exposed cleavage and jacaranda trees — it took place on a tropical island) before abandoning the project.

But writing those pages taught me an important lesson: Don't select a topic or form for your book just because you think it is commercially viable and will make you a lot of money. If you do, you won't be enthusiastic about the book, and that lack of enthusiasm will show through in your writing, as it did in my romance novel.

On the other hand, if you are passionate about your topic, your enthusiasm will show through in your writing. The book will be easier and more fun to write. The final product will be much better in quality. If there is a wide enough audience, it may become a best-seller. If not, you may still sell thousands of copies and receive praise from book reviewers and your readers.

The second book project I started working on upon graduation from college was a trivia book on comic book superheroes, written in quiz form. For example: What are the six types of kryptonite? (green, red, blue, white, gold, jewel.) What was Spider-Man's major in college? (physics.)

I wrote a short manuscript and, having no contacts in publishing, and no knowledge of the publishing business, sent it to editors at various paperback publishers with a cover letter. It was rejected by all. I gave up, and put it in a drawer.

Years later, when I was cleaning out some files, I came across the manuscript. I was going to throw it out, but saying "What the heck?," I mailed it to my literary agent with a note saying, "Do you think you can do anything with this?"

I expected no reply. But six weeks later, she called and said, "I have sold the comic book trivia book to a publisher." I was so shocked, I was speechless. The book, *Comic Book Heroes: 1,101 Trivia Questions About America's Favorite Superheroes From the Atom to the X-Men*, was published by Citadel Press in 1996.

The only sad note for me was that my father, who watched me enjoy comic books since age 8, would have loved to see me publish this book. My first author's copy arrived in the mail on the day of his funeral.

The second lesson learned from this experience was: A book idea that doesn't sell now might sell later. If you get rejected by publishers, don't throw away or forget about the book proposal. File it, and make a note to take another look at it in 6 or 12 months. Sometimes you have success on the second or third try because the timing is right. Other times, you see the idea from a fresh perspective, rewrite it, and make the sale with the revised book proposal. When asked to give a speech to the graduating class at Oxford, Winston Churchill, a great writer, stood up, said only three words — "Never give up" — and sat back down. These three words are good advice for authors who want to sell book proposals to publishers.

The third lesson learned: Every book published gives you a credential that can lead to more book contracts in the same field.

I enjoyed writing the comic book trivia book. It was fun to research and easy to write. After it came out, I thought about doing trivia books on other topics in a similar format.

I was always a big Star Trek fan. This resulted in two books with HarperCollins, *The Ultimate Unauthorized Star Trek Quiz Book* and *Why You Should Never Beam Down in a Red Shirt*. As publishers began to see me as a writer of popular culture trivia, I received several more contracts along this line including *What's Your Frasier I.Q.?*, a quiz book on the TV show Frasier.

Books about hobbies can be how-to, money-making, reference, specialized, or general information. Taking tropical fish, for example, you could write *How To Keep Tropical Fish* (How-to), *How To Breed Tropical Fish For Fun And Profit* (money-making), *An Illustrated Guide To Aquarium Fish* (reference), *Care And Breeding Of Fancy Guppies* (specialized), or *Your First Fish Tank* (general).

Notice that the first 6 methods on this list involve you, the author, having some special insight, experience, or information on the topic of your book. "Choose a category to write to," advises Joy Beck in *New Writer's Magazine* (December, 1995, p. 16). "Make your choice something that you have had some experience in dealing with."

Author and publisher Dan Poynter concurs: "Write about something in which you are a participant. The world needs more books written by writers who are also experts, not writers who are journalists."

"Concentrate on the area that interests you, and if you're not an expert now, you may become one," writes Tom Peeler in *The Writer* (July, 1995). "And even if the area of interest still requires consultation with recognized professionals, specialization will allow you to develop regular sources and will give you credibility with them."

Adds novelist Donna Levin, "One of the most marvelous things about writing is that nothing in your life is wasted." Almost every experience you've lived through, every piece of knowledge you've acquired, can be used somewhere in your writing.

One of Gary Larson's Far Side cartoons shows an author autographing his book at a book signing. The caption reads, "After being frozen in ice for 10,000 years, Thag promotes his autobiography." The title of the book: *It Was Very Cold and I Couldn't Move*. Obviously, no publisher expects you to have 10,000 years of experience in your subject matter. But writing about something you know, have experienced, or have achieved is one route to coming up with a book idea a publisher will buy from you.

### 7. COLLECT TIDBITS OF SCATTERED INFORMATION AND COMPILE THEM INTO A BOOK

Are you interested in a specific field of knowledge or study?

And are you the type who constantly clips articles and collects tidbits of information on your topic? If so, you can convert this passion for information by compiling your collected knowledge into book form.

Example: For a while, I became fascinated with all the toll-free consumer helplines and hotlines I saw advertised, giving free information on everything from AIDS prevention to gardening tips to stock market quotes. I became an obsessive collector of these numbers, clipping articles and writing down 800 numbers I heard on radio and saw on TV. Finally, I compiled them into a book, *Information Hotline U.S.A.*, published by New American Library.

Another example: A friend, Don Hauptman, is obsessed by language in general and word-play in particular. Don is a collector of information, and began collecting acronyms (e.g., DNA, LSD, scuba, laser). When his collection got large enough, he turned it into a book on acronyms, *Acronymania*, published by Dell.

## 8. Find and Fill A Need or Gap in The Reader's Knowledge

An excellent way of finding marketable ideas is to talk with people and find out what they want and need to know, then write a book to satisfy that information need.

For example, an attorney with good negotiating skills heard many clients telling him that they too wished they had good negotiating skills and would like help becoming better negotiators. The attorney became a millionaire by writing and selling books, audio and videotape programs, seminars, and training sessions in negotiating skills.

Working as a business consultant, I saw there were dozens of books on sales, but almost nothing on how to generate leads for salespeople. I proposed *The Lead Generation Handbook*, which sold to Amacom, the publishing division of the American

Management Association.

Another example: When we moved out of New York City and bought a home in the suburbs, we knew nothing about plumbing, electricity, gardening, cars, aluminum siding, roofing, or the dozens of other things every homeowner eventually becomes familiar with. I thought, "Why not do a book that will be an 'instruction manual' for first-time homeowners?"

I wrote a proposal for a book titled *The Homeowner's Survival Guide*. No one was interested, and I put the proposal away in a file and forgot about it. Several years later, a major publisher — one for whom I've now written several books — came out with such a book with the exact same title. Another lesson learned...pay attention to your own gut feelings. Had I kept trying with this book, as I advise you to do, it might very well have sold within a year or so. But I gave up on it, and now another author's name is on the cover.

## 9. WRITE WHAT INTERESTS YOU

In addition to finding out what interests other people, an excellent source of ideas is what interests you. You are a curious, intelligent, creative human being, constantly thinking and wondering about the world around you. Chances are what interests you will interest many other people, too.

I recommend you keep a notebook, file folder, or computer file labeled "book ideas," and whenever an idea for a book comes to mind, write it down and save it. In chapter 4 we will analyze the sales potential of these ideas carefully, judging them in the cold light of day. But creating ideas and analyzing/assessing ideas are two separate and distinct activities, and should not overlap. Don't hold your creativity back or stifle your imagination. Let the ideas flow, and right now, get them all down on paper. Later you can decide which won't work and which merit further effort.

*EXAMPLE:* I'm a big Stephen King fan. And I know there are many of us. (If this were not the case, there would not be a

Stephen King Book Club, and King would not be the best-selling novelist of all time.) Having written the TV and comic book quiz books, I naturally thought of doing a quiz book on Stephen King. My agent promptly sold it to Kensington Books, a paperback publisher in New York City.

### 10. Take An Existing Topic and Target It To A Specific Audience

A common situation is the author who wants to write a book on a specific topic but finds the field overcrowded.

This happens to all of us: You get an idea for a book, get excited about it. But then you visit the bookstore and find two shelves full of books on the same topic ... books that seem very much like yours. You become discouraged by the competition, give up, and drop the idea. Don't! You can still write that book. You just need a fresh slant, angle, or hook.

One of the easiest and most successful methods of coming up with a fresh idea in an area where there is lots of competition is to target your book toward a specific audience or segment of the market.

For example, a woman seminar leader told me she wanted to write a book on presentation skills, but was afraid to try because so many books already exist. She mentioned at one point that she trained mainly women. "Do women making presentations in the business world face a different set of challenges than men do?" I asked. "Of course," she replied. "Then," I continued, "the title of your book should be *Presentation Skills For Women.*"

In the same way, I wanted to write a book on selling, but found the market overcrowded. Since my experience is in selling services vs. products, I offered Henry Holt & Company a book on *Selling Your Services*. It was published in 1991 and has sold decently — well over 25,000 copies so far.

**EXERCISE:** Using these 10 idea-producing techniques, come up with at least half a dozen potential ideas for books. List them on a sheet of paper in priority order, starting with the idea you like best, followed by the ideas that are less interesting to you. Then go on to chapter 4 for tips on how to evaluate the commercial viability of your book ideas.

# CHAPTER 4

# EVALUATING YOUR BOOK IDEA

Coming up with ideas for books is fun and exciting. However, the fact is, not every book idea you or I have would make a good book: some would, others would not. Why is that so?

➤ Some ideas have been overworked. The field is too crowded, and the odds are against another book on the same topic doing well. You may want to write a diet book, but unless your diet is radically different or better than the others already published, why would a publisher do yet another diet book, with so many in the bookstores to choose from?

➤ For other ideas, the market is too small: There are not enough people who would buy the book to pay back the author and publisher for the time and money expended to produce it. I long to write a history of chemical engineering (I'm a chemical engineer by training), but the number of people who would buy such a book is too small to interest most publishers.

➤ Other topics are important and valuable but do not have sufficient depth to justify a full-length book, and would be more appropriate for an article, speech, seminar, booklet, special report, or monograph.

For instance, a friend of mine, a graphic artist, complained to me that clients are not interested in quality and craftsmanship any more; all they care about is whether the design was done on a Macintosh, whether it's in Quark XPress or PageMaker, how quickly the designer can make changes, and whether he or she can supply the printer with a disk.

This immediately put a book title into my head — *The Death of Craft.* The book would explore how, in all facets of trade, people in today's sped-up society value speed, efficiency, and customer service over quality and the work itself; and how, as a result, the successful people today are good businesspeople rather than skilled artisans.

I like the idea. But is there enough for a whole book there? And even if there is, why would someone read and buy this book? "Social issue" books, unless written on a hot news topic or by a controversial personality or celebrity, are a hard sell, attracting a limited audience of serious readers. I may pursue this, but with the understanding that the odds are against making the sale ... and if I sell it, the odds are against the book making a lot of money.

It is important to evaluate realistically the sales potential of your book idea before you spend time and effort researching the topic, creating a content outline, writing a book proposal, and trying to sell the book to an agent or publisher. Otherwise, you could spend years developing a manuscript no one will publish or buy. Evaluating the idea in advance of doing this work saves time and effort, and increases your chances of making a sale.

Publishers evaluate potential book ideas, proposals, and manuscripts using five key questions. By using the same set of questions to evaluate your idea, you not only gain a more realistic view of its potential, but have a better chance of having your proposal pass the publishing house's review and selection process.

Here are the five key questions editors will ask themselves when evaluating your book idea, and suggestions on how you can evaluate the answers accurately on your own:

## EVALUATION CRITERION #1:
### "IS THIS A BOOK OR A MAGAZINE ARTICLE?"

For most nonfiction books, the finished manuscript will be 250 to 300 double-spaced typed pages.

A typeset page in a trade paperback or hardcover book has approximately 400 words on it. Therefore, a 200-page book contains approximately 80,000 words.

As you may know, a double-spaced manuscript page is approximately 250 words long. Dividing 80,000 words by 250 words per manuscript page, we get 320 manuscript pages for a 200-page published book. Subtract 20 pages for the "front matter" (acknowledgments, dedication, table of contents), index, and author's bio, and you must write 300 double-spaced manuscript pages on your PC, word processor, or typewriter to complete an average-sized book.

Of course, there will always be books that are longer and shorter. My book, *The "I Hate Kathie Lee Gifford" Book*, is a tiny volume — barely a hundred pages, with a small trim size and large type. On the other end of the spectrum, some reference books are a thousand pages or more (my *Advertising Manager's Handbook* is 800 pages).

If there's a reason to make your book extremely short or extremely long, you'll have to explain it to the publisher in your book proposal, under the "Format" section (see chapter 6). But unless there's a compelling reason to do a very short or long book, aim for the standard-size 200 pages or so. "I don't see people my age having the attention span to read a 1,000-page book," says 24-year-old Barnes & Noble employee Matthew Reed (Daily News, February 13, 1996). "Two hundred pages, maybe. But a thousand? That's asking a little too much."

If anything, I predict books will get shorter (125 to 175 pages) rather than longer, to reflect our shorter attention spans and the information-gathering habits of the PC/CD-ROM/MTV/ Nintendo/Sega generation. Panning a book he was reviewing, Ambrose Bierce wrote, "The covers of this book are too far apart" (as reported in American Scholar, Spring 1996). Make sure the same can't be said about your book.

Take a good, hard look at the book ideas on the list you created from the previous chapter. Can you really write 250 to 300 informative, entertaining, fresh pages on this topic? If not, the idea is probably not worth pursuing.

If you cannot easily fill the required number of pages, re-examine your idea. Perhaps the subject does not warrant book-length treatment. Or perhaps it does, but there is simply not enough information available to fill a book.

You will have to create a detailed outline (see chapter 5) showing what goes in the book as part of your proposal. If you cannot demonstrate via such an outline that you have sufficient material for a full-length book, the editor will probably reject your proposal.

It's fun to write a book when information is plentiful; miserable to write one when you are stretching to come up with text and padding every chapter. So if you cannot convince yourself that there's enough material for a book in your idea, drop it and go on to another topic.

Sometimes an idea strikes you, but once you start writing, you rapidly run out of material. Several years ago, when the recession of the late 1980s and early 1990s began to become severe, I had what I thought was a great idea for a book — *Recession-Proof Business Strategies — How to Market and Sell ANY Product or Service in a Soft Economy."* Timely? Yes. And needed.

I sat down to write. When I was done, I had 5,000 words (20 double-spaced typed pages) — not the 80,000 words needed to fill a 200-page business book. Solution? I self-published *"Recession-Proof Business Strategies"* as a 16-page pamphlet, and sold more than 3,000 copies at $7 each, all through mailing one publicity release to 600 newspapers and magazines. Not a book, but a very profitable venture, grossing $21,000 for a manuscript equivalent to a long magazine article.

Recently my sometimes co-author Gary Blake and I came up with what we thought was a great book title: *How To Have A Mid-life Crisis--At Any Age!* But when we sat down to do the outline, we couldn't think of anything to put in the book. We still can't. Any suggestions?

## EVALUATION CRITERION #2:
### "WHO IS THE AUDIENCE ... AND HOW MANY OF THEM ARE THERE?"

Who will read your book? And why? How many of them are there? Do they go to bookstores? If not, how would you reach them?

Publishers would love to sell a million copies of every book, but they recognize that books with truly "universal" market appeal are few and far between. You've got to show that your book is of interest to a specific, identifiable segment of the market — e.g., gardeners, small business owners, single parents, teens, science fiction fans, Windows users, corporate managers, homeowners, investors, Internet "newbies" (first-time Internet users), senior citizens, engineers, soap opera fans — and that this market segment is large enough to warrant publication of the book.

The idea is to pick a market that's targeted enough so that the book can be made specific to the interests of those readers, yet not so narrow that the market is too small and limits sales potential. How do you make this distinction?

One successful literary agent told me, "Publishers will buy the pie or a slice, but not a slice of a slice." What this means is that they will buy a book with broad mass appeal or one that goes to a decent-sized segment of the market, but not a book that is targeted to an audience so small and specialized that sales volume would not justify the cost of publication.

As an example, there are many general books on the topic of selling that appeal to just about every businessperson who sells (the pie). I was able to sell a book, *Selling Your Services*, that targeted only those who sell services as opposed to products (a slice). I was able to make that sale because, by segmenting the market, the book would have more appeal to service sellers than a generic book on selling.

However, I doubt any mainstream publisher would buy a book on SELLING GARDEN SUPPLIES. That's too narrow — a "slice of a slice" — and there are too few potential readers to justify publication. It could be sold mail order in pamphlet form to garden store owners.

How big must the potential market be for a publisher to show interest in a book? There's no hard and fast rule. But consider this: Most publishers plan on selling at least 5,000 copies of your book, and most hope to sell 10,000 or more. A book selling fewer than 5,000 copies is generally considered financially unsuccessful.

Let's assume that you can capture 5 percent of the market with your title. To sell 5,000 books, you would need a minimum market of 100,000 potential readers. Therefore, if your book appeals to a specialized market, you should be able to demonstrate to the publisher that there are at least 100,000 of them. If the publisher isn't convinced of this, they will be unlikely to make you an offer.

Another example: After starting a freelance writing business from scratch and building my gross billings to more than $150,000 a year, I knew other writers would want to learn my techniques for making more money as a freelancer, and decided to write a how-to book telling them how to do so (published as *Secrets of a Freelance Writer* by Henry Holt & Company in New York City).

But writers represent a small, specialized audience. Would a publisher produce a book for such a narrow segment of the home-based business market?

To prove an adequate market existed, I called the two major writer's magazines, *Writer's Digest* and *The Writer,* and discovered their combined circulation was more than 320,000. This is the figure I used in my book proposal. The proposal sold, and *Secrets of a Freelance Writer,* although aimed at a limited market, has sold respectably — more than 25,000 copies to date.

With some book ideas, it is difficult to define the precise target market or research hard numbers for this audience. For example, a student in one of my writing seminars at the Learning Annex in New York City wanted to write a nonfiction book on the children of preachers and how the kids are affected by their father's or mother's profession.

This is a serious "social issue" book and, as such, would be difficult to sell. Yet it's a solid topic that would probably make a good book appealing to a limited audience of people who read such books.

The problem is proving an audience. It's almost impossible to determine how many people are the children of preachers. And even if you could, this isn't really the market for the book: Since it's journalistic, and not instructional or self help, it appeals to people who read social issue books, not particularly preacher's kids.

When you have a book idea without a well-targeted market, or when the size of the market is difficult to pinpoint accurately, the tactic to use is as follows: Find a book similar to your idea. Call the publisher or check one of the industry journals (such as *Publisher's Weekly*; see appendix H) to find out how many copies have sold. Then compare your book to the published book. You are implying that (a) your book is like book X, (b) book X sold a lot of copies, and (c) therefore the same audience that bought book X will buy your book.

While this is not necessarily true, it's a believable logic that seems convincing. For instance, if I wrote and was trying to sell a quirky romance novel with literary pretensions, I'd compare it to *The Bridges of Madison County* and say, "My book appeals to the millions of readers who eagerly bought and read *The Bridges of Madison County*."

It's easiest if the book you are comparing to is currently on the best-seller list, because you can simply note that the book is a best-seller, and publishers will be impressed. If the book you are comparing to is not a best-seller, getting sales figures may be difficult. You might look for articles or reviews about the book or its author that give sales figures, or you can call the public relations department of the publishing house and see whether they will share sales figures with you.

If this doesn't work, take a look at the copyright page in the book. You will see numbers at the bottom of the page as follow: 1 2 3 4 5 6 7 8 9 10. These indicate the "printing" of the book, meaning how many times it has been reprinted. This is an indicator of sales, as a book that has been reprinted must have good  enough sales to warrant a publisher's going back to press and printing more copies.

If the copyright page says 2 3 4 5 6 7 8 9 10, the book is in its second printing, and you should say "this book is in its second printing" in your proposal to the publisher. If the copyright page says 6 7 8 9 10, the book is in its sixth printing. This is an easy way to demonstrate a book has decent sales.

## Evaluation Criterion #3:
### "What's the competition, and how is my book different or better?"

Most topics you will want to write a book on have been done before. The trick is not necessarily to come up with something completely new, but to put a new twist or slant on an old topic.

If you are aware of other books on your topic, don't try to hide this fact from potential publishers and hope they won't find out about the competition. They will.

In fact, not acknowledging and dealing with competition in your proposal will hurt you: The publisher will feel that you do not know what is available in your field, which undermines your credibility as a knowledgeable expert.

> *You have your best shot at making a sale if there is limited competition and you can clearly differentiate your book from these other titles.*

Having no competition is not necessarily a good sign. You may think it means you've hit upon a unique idea no one has thought of. And perhaps you have.

But that's not likely. If the idea is so hot, someone else must have thought of it. So why are there no books on it? Perhaps there's no market, or the subject is not something that appeals to book readers. As sales expert Paul Karasik has said, if nobody else is doing it, you have to question whether there's even a need.

Likewise, too much competition is not good. Fields can be overcrowded; subjects can be overdone. If you find more than six or seven books on the market, recently published by major publishing houses, that seem identical or pretty similar to yours, you may want to rethink the project ... and either pursue another idea or more clearly differentiate yours from the pack.

When I am researching competition, I am happy if I find two to six other books that are similar to mine, but not so close that I can't easily and clearly differentiate mine in my proposal. Two to six competing titles means there clearly is a market for books on the subject, yet the market is not so overcrowded that there isn't room for one more good book.

The first step in researching competition is to check a directory called *Books In Print*, available in your local library. *Books In Print* lists all books currently in print by subject, title, and author.

Check your subject in *Books In Print*, and also check for titles identical or similar to yours. Photocopy these pages from the directory or copy down the information in a notebook. You'll also want to check the companion volume, *Forthcoming Books In Print,* which lists books soon to be published.

Now, working with this list, eliminate books that are self-published or done by small unknown publishing houses. Also eliminate books with copyright (publication) dates of 5 years ago or older.

What remains is recent (published within the last 5 years) books published by major publishing houses. Get copies from the library or bookstores, or order from the publisher.

*NOTE:* If you don't want to buy the books and the library does not have them, go to one or more of the bigger chain bookstores in your town. Bring a notepad and pen or mini tape recorder. Find the books; take notes on the content and other information about the books. Naturally bookstores don't like this (they would prefer you to buy the book), but if you are quiet and inconspicuous, you can get away with it and save yourself some money. The new superstores, in fact, encourage extensive browsing and in-store reading (although not for this particular purpose).

The information you should collect on competing titles (books similar to your proposed topic) is as follows:

- Title and subtitle
- Author
- Publisher and city where publisher is located (e.g., New York: McGraw-Hill)
- Cover price
- Date of publication (copyright date)
- Is the book a hardcover, trade paperback, or mass market paperback?
- Number of pages
- Overview of the book's contents (one or two sentences)
- Any weaknesses, flaws, or faults you spot in the presentation and treatment of subject matter e.g., failure to cover a vital topic, lack of illustrations, poor organization, poor writing, etc.

In the written proposal for your book, you will list and describe each of these books, highlight their inherent weaknesses or flaws, and explain, with specifics, how your book is different or better. For example:

> *Tested Advertising Methods* by John Caples (Englewood Cliffs, NJ: Prentice Hall, hardcover, 292 pages, 1989, $24.95). A classic book on how to write effective headlines and body copy. Good information. However, the book focuses mainly on space ads and mainly on mail order selling. Other selling methods and formats are not covered.

For now, the important thing is to research and understand the competition and the market. Are you offering a new twist or slant on a popular topic? Or has it been done so many times that there is no need for yet another book on it?

If your idea looks to truly be a "first," is it possible that there are no other books on the topic because it's not a subject people want a book on? Or are you ahead of the pack, offering publishers a unique and hot topic? More important, how can you prove to them that interest in your topic is strong and a book is needed? The answer is to demonstrate a large market of eager and interested buyers, as discussed earlier in this chapter.

## EVALUATION CRITERION #4: "WHY WOULD SOMEONE PAY $14.95 FOR THIS?"

The average hardcover book costs about $24; the average trade paperback, about $14.95. For the book to sell, people have to be willing to invest their money to buy it, and their time to read it.

This means your proposed book must satisfy one of the following criteria:

**A.** The story it tells is so entertaining that people would pay $14.95 for it. That is, it's interesting to people and fun to read. It arouses their curiosity. Gets their attention. They want to know more. The subject captures their imagination. Celebrity biographies fill this need.

Example: Most TV shows have viewers, but Star Trek has fans. Given the power of Trek mania, I came up with *The Ultimate Unauthorized Star Trek Quiz Book*, published by HarperCollins. Trekkers and others who watched the series read the book for pure enjoyment. It's fun for them to test their knowledge, and the trivia brings back fond memories of favorite episodes. The book has sold more than 45,000 copies.

**B.** The information contained in your book, if properly applied, will produce benefits for the reader; and the value of these benefits is greater than the investment required to buy and read the book.

Key benefits sought by readers include: losing weight, looking good, making money, saving money, staying healthy, becoming fit, having more sex, having better relationships, saving time, having more leisure, doing better on the job, being successful, finding love, avoiding pain, and being happy.

People want benefits. The greater the desirability and perceived value of the benefits you offer, the more appealing your book. For example, the cover story of a recent issue of *Money Magazine* was, "How to turn $10,000 into $25,000 in 5 Years." Getting people to buy a magazine (or book) with that title is not a problem, since the reader gets a potential return of $15,000 profit on an investment of a few dollars.

Example: The average writer in the United States earns $25,000 a year. The subtitle of my book, *Secrets of a Freelance Writer: How to Make $85,000 a Year*, promises to tell them how to triple their income. That's a powerful benefit, and probably why the book sold more than 25,000 copies.

*C.* The book contains reference information that is important or is not easily available elsewhere. A good example would be a cookbook of low-fat recipes for readers with high-blood pressure and others who must restrict fat in their diet. Another example: A directory of where to apply for government grants.

As discussed earlier, there are numerous toll-free hotlines that offer free products, free information, and other assistance to consumers. But unless you happen to hear one mentioned in a news report or read about it in a magazine, you won't even know it's there. My New American Library Book, *Information Hotline*, solved this problem by offering a directory of such phone hotlines published as an inexpensive trade paperback. I doubt anyone read the book through from cover to cover. But thousands of people bought it because it contained information they felt they might need some day and would like to have handy just in case. One could argue that just one piece of information or help received from one phone call to just one of the hotlines could pay back the cost of the book several times over, which is one reason why people will buy such a book.

If your book does not meet any of the above criteria — and this is often the case — you will have a more difficult time finding a publisher.

Many ideas which you as a writer find intellectually engaging are a difficult sell because they do not have strong appeal to others, and the information is not directly applicable or useful.

For example, I am trained as a chemical engineer, and would like to write a book about the history of the chemical engineering profession. But to most people, even other chemical engineers, this is a dry subject; I do not think most chemical engineers would want to spend their weekends reading about chemical engineering.

Chemical engineers do buy nonfiction books, but these are references useful in their engineering work. The information in a history of chemical engineering may be interesting, but does it help them do their jobs or make them more successful in their work? No. Therefore, I have chosen not to pursue this book, based on a frank evaluation of the book's potential. If I can't let the idea drop, one strategy would be to approach the American Institute of Chemical Engineers and see if they want to publish it for their membership and a limited additional readership.

## EVALUATION CRITERION #5: "WHY YOU?"

Okay. The publisher likes your book idea. There's a ready market that's easy to reach. Your book offers useful information, and there's plenty of material for a meaty text. Given this favorable reaction to your proposal, the editors will then say, "Okay, we want a book like this. But is this author (meaning *you*) the best-qualified to write it?"

If the publisher decides they like the book but not you, is it possible they may do it with another author? Yes. Does this mean publishers are stealing ideas — taking proposals from authors and hiring other writers to create the books? No. "Publishers do not steal people's ideas," says publisher Jack Tracy. "We're all much too busy, and we generally have more books on our hands than we can publish."

The fact is, publishers get many proposals on the same subject in a given year that are pretty similar to one another. Given that they like the idea, whether you make the sale then comes down to whether you seem able and qualified to write the book — and whether you are more qualified than other would-be authors with similar proposals. Timing, of course, is another factor: Your proposal may cross the editor's desk just when she had it in mind to do such a book, and the immediacy of having your material at hand gives you the edge in making the sale.

This was demonstrated during a luncheon meeting my sometimes co-author Gary Blake and I had with an editor at New American Library. She had just bought our proposal for our book, *How To Promote Your Own Business*, and wanted to discuss it.

I had thought our idea — a marketing, advertising, and promotion guide for small business — was unique. But then she casually remarked, "You know, the fact that you guys are in PR and advertising (Gary had a PR agency at the time; I was and still am a freelance advertising copywriter) swayed me. I get a lot of proposals for *'How to Promote Your Own Business'* from writers, but you guys are experts." We were shocked to discover we had not provided her with the "exclusive" we thought we had.

There are three types of credentials editors will look at in determining your potential as an author: expert credentials, writing credentials, and media credentials.

If you have good credentials, great! That's a plus. But if not, don't worry. Part of the technique of "book proposalmanship" is knowing how to take your limited credentials and experience and make them seem much more than they really are — without lying, of course.

Here are the three types of credentials along with strategies to make yourself more credible in all three areas:

**A. *EXPERT CREDENTIALS.*** You want to write a nonfiction book on topic X. The publisher wants to know, "What makes you think you know enough about topic X to write a book on it? Why should readers find what you say, your information and ideas, credible?"

The more credentials you have that position you as an expert in your subject matter, the better. Such credentials can include:

- Job or business experience
- Life experience
- Education, courses completed, degrees
- Skills, background, knowledge
- Awards, patents, honors, publications
- Membership in professional and trade associations.

For example, if you are going to write *How To Start And Open A Successful Restaurant*, publishers would be more likely to buy this book from you if you had in fact started your own restaurant. Or at least had worked in a restaurant or as a consultant to the field.

If you lack in-depth expert credentials, there are several things you can do to make yourself seem more established. One is to join the key associations in your field, then list membership as a credential in your bio.

Another is to become a participant in your topic, even on a small scale. For example, if you want to write a book on *How To Pass Civil Service Tests,* you should take and pass such a test. If you want to write a book on *How To Start A Mail Order Business*, you should start a small home-based mail order business as a hobby.

When you write your bio in your book proposal, present your credentials in a straightforward, positive manner, without apology or explanation. For example, in our book *How To Sell Your House, Co-op, Or Condo*, my wife's bio reads, "Amy Bly is a licensed real estate agent in New Jersey." We didn't feel the need to add that she got the license because she won a free course in real estate as a prize at a Chinese auction, and that she has never actually worked as an agent. And the publisher never asked. But the license was an extra credential that made us more appealing as a team to write a book on this subject.

**B. WRITING CREDENTIALS.** If you have written other books, say so. This tells the publisher that you at least have demonstrated your ability to write a book.

If you have published in magazines, say so and list a number of them. This demonstrates your ability to write as well as your ability to sell what you write.

If you haven't written books or magazine articles, list any other relevant major writing experience that sounds professional or semi-professional. This would include articles for trade journals or local newspapers (even if you didn't get paid for them), ghostwriting speeches for your boss, whatever.

Do not list amateur accomplishments such as having entered three of your poems in a poetry contest or winning a prize for best short story in your local writer's group.

**C. MEDIA CREDENTIALS.** Some publishers promote books by booking you, the author, on radio and TV shows. If the publisher feels this is a good strategy for promoting your proposed book, they will be more inclined to publish it if you are someone who is good at doing such interviews.

If you have appeared as a guest on any radio or TV shows, let the publisher know, naming the shows and stations. This will reassure them that you know what to do and are indeed promotable as a personality.

Make the most of even minor media appearances. For instance, if you were interviewed by the local college on the student radio station, or even did a show there while you were a student, say "I have appeared on several radio stations including WRUR." The editor will never know WRUR is the student station of the University of Rochester in Rochester, New York.

If you haven't made any media appearances, don't worry about it. Of the three types of credentials, media credentials are the least important factor in the publisher making a decision whether to publish your book. It's simply not that big a deal.

If you do have the opportunity to be interviewed by the media, take it. For years, I shunned radio interviews, viewing them as a waste of time, and let my coauthor, Gary Blake, do all the radio shows, which he eagerly sought and enjoyed. I thought I was being smart. But when it came time to write books on my own, I had no media credentials, because it had been Gary, not me, who did all the radio talk shows.

I still don't like doing media interviews — they take up valuable writing time, and I am not as convinced as others that they sell a lot of books — but I do them, because each is an added credential I can use in my author's bio. For instance, a few years ago, I did a five-minute segment with CNBC on real estate, promoting a real estate book I coauthored with my wife. Now in my bio I say "Bob has appeared on radio and TV." I don't mention that CNBC is the only TV I've ever done (except for a brief on-air editorial at a local TV station in Rochester, New York); there's no need or reason for me to do so.

**EXERCISE:** Using these five questions, evaluate the ideas on your "idea list" produced after reading chapter 3. After completion, you should be left with one or two ideas that "pass the test" and are potential big sellers. If not, repeat the exercises in chapter 3 and chapter 4 until you have at least one feasible book idea you are ready to take to the next step.

# CHAPTER 5

# CREATING THE CONTENT OUTLINE

The content outline is a detailed outline for your book. Creating a content outline offers several advantages:

➤ It tells you whether you have enough material for a full-length book. If you can't come up with a detailed outline, then you probably can't write a detailed book.

➤ It communicates to the publisher that you know your topic and have enough information to write a full-length book.

➤ Since every proposal must have a content outline, doing one now saves you time later when you are writing your book proposal.

➤ It saves you time doing the book. The major sections of your content line become the chapter headings of your books; the major points in each section become chapter subheads. Once you have a complete content outline, you've already done the hard part — organizing your book. Writing the book then becomes simply a matter of filling in some text under each major point/subhead.

➤ Doing the content outline lets you know exactly how many pages you have to write and makes it easier to create a schedule for completion of the book.

## ORGANIZING YOUR BOOK INTO CHAPTERS

As discussed, the average nonfiction book is 200 pages. The average typeset book page is approximately 400 words, so 400 words per book page times 200 book pages equals an 80,000-word book. The average double-spaced typed manuscript page from your typewriter or word processor contains 250 words. Therefore the manuscript for an 80,000-word book will be approximately 320 double-spaced typed pages.

Your book should have no fewer than 9 or 10 chapters and no more than 20 or so. I like to shoot for 15 chapters, but the number depends on the best way to organize your material and how many subtopics must be covered. If you have 15 chapters in your book, and the complete manuscript must be 320 pages, then chapters should be about 21 double-spaced typed pages, or a little over 5,000 words, each. (Actually, they can be a little less because of the "front matter" and "back matter" in your book. The front matter includes introductory pages such as the title page, table of contents, dedication, acknowledgments, and copyright page. The back matter includes the author's biography, appendices and the index.)

In your content outline, chapter heads show major content and flow of thinking. Underneath each major chapter heading, 5-6 bulleted points — or two to three short paragraphs — per chapter show depth of knowledge and detail.

## WRITING YOUR CONTENT OUTLINE

First write down all major subjects to be covered in the book, each of which will have a chapter devoted to it. You can do this on your PC or using index cards or sheets of paper.

Next, put these in some sort of logical order. If there is no logical order, just put them in the sequence you feel is best.

Now, under each, start jotting secondary topics — points that you will want to cover in the chapter on that topic. Many of these will become actual chapter subheads when you write the manuscript; others may just be discussed within the text. Here is an example from the proposal for my book *How To Promote Your Own Business:*

CHAPTER 2: PLANNING YOUR PROMOTIONS
Writing a business plan
Target marketing: Define your customers...
-by geographic location
-by age, income, sex, and other demographics
-by business and job title
Questions to ask when planning promotions:
-How can I reach my prospects?
-What do I want to say to them?
-What is the best way to say it?
-How do I want them to respond?

Where do you get the ideas and information to put into your content outline? From a combination of your own knowledge of the subject and research. The research can be a combination of secondary sources (library research) and primary sources (interviews). You should also look at the table of contents in published books dealing with your subject, to make sure you haven't left out any key chapter topics or points of information.

Your finished content outline will have 10 to 20 chapters, with 5 to 6 or more bullet points per chapter. If you feel you can write three to five double-spaced pages on each of the bullet points, you have enough information to fill a full-length nonfiction book.

Once you have completed your content outline, you are ready to go to the next step, *writing the book proposal*. Save your content outline now as a separate document on your word processor or PC, if you use one. It will be helpful later when you write your book and book proposal.

## SAMPLE CONTENT OUTLINES

Here are the content outlines as presented in book proposals for two of my books. Although yours need not be this detailed, my feeling is that, for most books, the more detail you have, the greater your chance of making the sale. And the easier it is to write the book once you get a contract from a publisher.

## SAMPLE ONE

*THE ELEMENTS OF COPYWRITING*
(Macmillan)

Table of Contents

Preface

Introduction

PART I: COPYWRITING PRINCIPLES

This section presents three chapters dealing with fundamentals of copywriting that apply to all formats.

CHAPTER 1: THE ELEMENTS OF PERSUASION
This chapter presents a series of guidelines for writing more persuasively. It includes:
* getting attention with "hooks" or "angles"
* usage of clever vs. direct wording
* how to sustain reader interest throughout a piece of copy
* how to make people want to buy your product, see your point of view, or respond to your communication
* how to avoid copywriting mistakes that can detract from your persuasiveness
* targeting features and benefits to the needs and concerns of your readers.

## CHAPTER 2: WRITING HEADLINES

Effective copy begins with attention-getting headlines. This chapter tells how to write powerful headlines and also presents different categories of headlines that have been proven to attract readership. Also identifies which types of headline (e.g., blind, pun, generic) to avoid.

## CHAPTER 3: BODY COPY

Tips and techniques for writing clear, concise, easy to understand body copy. Emphasis is on understanding when copywriting can and should violate the rules of conventional English composition as well as when it should adhere to them (e.g., such issues as starting a sentence with a conjunction, sentence fragments, unconventional use of punctuation).

## CHAPTER 4: INCREASING READERSHIP AND RESPONSE

Most advertising has three goals: to be read, to be memorable, and to generate response. This chapter contains techniques for achieving all three objectives. Readers will learn:

* how to make any subject interesting to your prospect
* how to present old information in a fresh way
* offers that get more people to respond to your copy
* more tricks of the trade

## PART II: COPYWRITING TASKS

## CHAPTER 5: PRINT ADS

Rules and principles for creating effective space advertisements for all media including:

* newspapers
* freestanding inserts
* magazines
* Yellow Pages
* other directories

The discussion covers all types of ads: full page, fractional, classified display, and classified.

## CHAPTER 6: DIRECT MAIL

Of all the copywriting forms, direct mail has the

largest set of established rules and guidelines because its response is so measurable and various approaches can be scientifically tested. This chapter covers techniques and strategies for writing effective direct mail including:

* outer envelopes
* sales letters
* brochures
* lift notes
* buck slips
* order forms
* self mailers
* postcards
* double postcards
* magalogs.

### CHAPTER 7: BROCHURES

The brochure is the most widely used of all promotional vehicles. Even companies that can't afford advertising or mailings have one or more brochures. This chapter presents rules for effective copywriting and design of brochures including:

* what to say on the front cover
* how to organize the three types of brochures (product, service, corporate)
* tips for writing more effective brochure copy
* how to illustrate and design your own brochures

The chapter will cover not only traditional brochures but such variations as "slim jims" and rack brochures, data sheets, fliers, circulars, booklets, and pamphlets.

### CHAPTER 8: CATALOGS

The catalog industry is a multibillion dollar business. This chapter covers all types of catalogs: consumer mail order, counter or point of purchase, and industrial. Topics include:

* how to write effective product descriptions
* merchandising and page layout
* most effective copy styles for catalog selling
* best photos and visuals to use

### CHAPTER 9: PRESS RELEASES

Publicity is the lowest-cost form of marketing, and the major promotional focus of many businesses, small and large. This chapter gives rules for writing publicity materials that editors will use and readers will respond to. Covers:

* Proper press release format
* Organization
* Style
* Themes, slants, and hooks
* Formats: press releases, press kits, backgrounders, public service announcements, others

## CHAPTER 10: AUDIO-VISUAL

Proper formats and techniques for writing audio-visual promotions including:

* TV commercials
* Infomercials
* Radio commercials
* Slide presentations
* Disk and CD-ROM presentations
* Multimedia presentations
* Videos

## CHAPTER 11: ON-LINE PROMOTIONS

Step-by-step guidelines on how to promote products and services on the Internet. Tells how to write and create:

* Home pages and web sites
* On-line advertisements
* Threads and messages

## CHAPTER 12: OTHER FORMATS

Rules and tips for writing promotions and documents not covered in previous chapters, including:

* newsletters
* company magazines
* employee communications
* package inserts and invoice stuffers
* manuals and instructions
* annual reports
* signs

## INDEX

## ABOUT THE AUTHORS

## SAMPLE TWO

### *HOW TO MAKE $50,000 OR MORE A YEAR WRITING*
(Writer's Digest Books — forthcoming)

### Chapter Outline

Preface

Over the years I have gotten hundreds of letters from *Writers Digest* subscribers telling me that my books, seminars, and *Writers Digest* articles have helped them increase their writing income dramatically. The preface could consist of excerpts from these letters. The excerpts would tell our readers: "You can make a lot of money writing — and this book can show you how."

#### INTRODUCTION

The introduction discusses the concept, purpose, and design of the book. Key points: (a) you can make more money writing, (b) there are four ways to do this, (c) in this book you will learn all four ways (write faster, write more, sell more, charge more).

### PART ONE: WRITING FASTER

The first section focuses on how to write faster. The logic is simple: If you can do a $100 writing job in four hours, you earn $25 an hour. If you can do it in a half hour, you earn $200 per hour. This section shows how to double, triple, or quadruple your writing speed and therefore your per hour earnings rate.

#### Chapter 1. Work Habits That Speed You Up

Fast writers have certain work habits that aid productivity. These habits will be discussed so readers can emulate them and improve their own pace. Topics to be covered include: setting your daily schedule; determining priorities; the three types of TO-DO lists every writer should keep; how to overcome procrastination and writer's block; how to make every hour of every day productive; best writing styles for fast writers; 10 steps to writing better and faster; quick editing tips; how to eliminate unnecessary activities that slow you down; eliminating bad habits that waste time; setting and achieving realistic production goals.

Chapter 2. Lucrative Assignments You Can Do
Rapidly and Easily

Fast writers tend to take on only those assignments they can complete quickly and avoid assignments that would take them a long time. Often pay is not related to the degree of difficulty or time needed for completion. This week, for example, I wrote a $3,500 script for one client, in one day, in the morning. A project for another client took me all of the next day and earned me only $400. By selecting the former and avoiding the latter, writers can do more work in less time ... and make more money in the process. This chapter tells what these assignments are, where to find them, why these projects can be done so rapidly, and how to get them (examples include service articles, quiz books, company newsletters, and certain types of business letters). Also included: factors that add time to complete writing projects — and factors that shorten time to completion.

Chapter 3. Quick Tips and Shortcuts to Help You Write
Better and Faster

This chapter presents a miscellany of tips, techniques, and methods you can use to write more in less time. These include:

* "early to bed, early to rise" — does keeping night-owl hours hurt writers' productivity?

* a surefire technique for maintaining peak energy throughout the day

* using sugar to boost energy

* the one-hour module method

* the index card method

* designing your work space for maximum productivity

* filing systems that work

* handling paperwork and work flow efficiently

* hard disk tips and techniques for better file management

* research and filing short cuts

* building your reference library

* using the Internet to cut your research time

* quick tips for copyediting and proofreading your work better and faster.


PART TWO: WRITING MORE

Writers can earn more money by producing more work. Writing faster can contribute to this. But there are other ways to get more done, including making best use of available time and increasing the percentage of billable vs.

nonbillable hours in the work week. Importantly, being prolific has to be a goal in itself; if you don't want to produce more, you probably won't.

### Chapter 4. Do you Really Want to be Prolific?

The primary reason most writers are not prolific is that they do not really desire it. Isaac Asimov wanted to write a lot of books, and so he designed his life to increase his output (this included doing focusing on topics on which he could produce books quickly and avoiding travel so he could spend most of his time in his study). Donald Hall, the poet, puts perfection before productivity, and so has revised at least one of his pieces more than 600 times! This chapter presents guidelines to help readers assess whether being prolific is important to them, and whether they are willing to do what is necessary to achieve superior productivity.

### Chapter 5. Work Habits of Prolific Writers

This chapter will take a look at some of the most prolific and productive writers and their work habits, showing readers how they might adapt these habits to their own writing. Georges Simeon, for example, limited his writing vocabulary to 2,000 words so he would not have to use a dictionary. Stephen King writes 1,500 words every day except his birthday, Christmas, and the Fourth of July. Sidney Sheldon and Barbara Cortland dictate drafts, then have their staff transcribe their novels for editing. The chapter will include more than a dozen case histories and work habits to emulate.

### Chapter 6. SureFire Techniques for Increasing Your Output 25% or More

Not every writer wants to be Isaac Asimov or Georges Simeon. This chapter focuses on helping the average writer achieve realistic incremental productivity increases without rearranging his or her life in the service of maximum productivity. By following these tips, almost every writer can increase output 10 to 25% within a few short weeks. Topics to be covered include: how to get an extra hour's work done every day ... how to prevent time-wasting interruptions ... saving time by interviewing subjects via phone, fax, or the Internet ... how to cut your travel time 50% or more ... getting work done while you daydream ... how to reduce the "agony" factor in your writing ... maximizing your productive time with "filler" assignments ... and more.

Chapter 7. Using Technology to Boost Your
Productivity — Computers, Software, Office Equipment,
and On-line Services

A nuts and bolts chapter on equipment you must have — and equipment you should have — to be a productive, prolific writer. Includes recommendations on Internet connections, on-line services, computers, modems, CD ROM drives, power supplies, surge protectors, fax machines, telephone systems, photocopiers, scanners, cellular phones, laptops, printers, beepers, and voice mail systems. Also includes recommendations on software including word processing, desktop publishing, spreadsheets, communications, graphics, virus protection, accounting, contact management, mailing list, dictionaries, reference CD ROMs, and grammar and spell checkers.

Chapter 8. Outsourcing — Hiring Others To
Work For You

Writers are basically selling their time, yet many writers fritter their valuable time away handling the most mundane tasks. A better strategy is to hire others to do nonwriting tasks for you, and concentrate on writing, selling, marketing, and customer service. This chapter gives the nuts and bolts of hiring temporary, part-time, and full-time help including both staff and independent contractors. I will show readers how I have increased my net profits by outsourcing a large number of nonwriting activities to outside firms. These activities include: faxing, typing, filing, library research, bookkeeping, tax preparation, photocopying, going to the post office, and selling and marketing.

PART THREE: INCREASING YOUR SALES

Writing faster and more can add to your writing income, but you'll do even better if you sell most of what you write.

Chapter 9. Queries and Proposals That Lock
In the Assignment

Writers spend a lot of uncompensated time proposing ideas, pursuing clients and editors, and selling themselves and their work. If the "closing rate" (percentage of clients and editors who give you the go ahead) is low, you will waste a lot of time, and therefore be less productive and profitable. This chapter shows how to write pitch letters, query letters, and proposals that sell 80% or more of your work to maximize your income and minimize time wasted. It will include samples of successful letters and proposals readers can use as models.

Chapter 10. How to Get Advance Contracts From Corporations and other Writing Clients

The writers who sell the largest percentage of their work are those that work on contract rather than on spec. This chapter covers: contracts, letters of agreement, purchase orders, deposits, advance payments, kill fees, billing and collections, monthly retainers, up-front time purchases, first rights and limited usage arrangements, buy outs, credit checking, terms, and legal considerations.

Chapter 11. The 4 R's: Making Money From Referrals, Repeat Business, Reprints, and Resales

In this chapter we explore four lucrative ways to make extra income from existing clients and writing projects: referrals, repeat orders, reprints, and resales.

* Referrals — the easiest way to get new clients is through referral from existing clients, prospects, colleagues, and even competitors. The book will show how to go about it.

* Repeat orders — most writers concentrate on new markets. Here's how to win lucrative ongoing repeat business from existing clients and editors. Repeat assignments are easier to get and take less time to complete.

* Reprints — I'll show the reader how I earn an extra $5,000 each year selling photocopied reprints of previously published articles I've written, via mail order.

* Resale — One writer earned an incredible $33,000 from one article selling it to 67 different publications. Here are tips for generating 5 to 10 times the revenue you now earn from each project.

PART FOUR: GETTING PAID BETTER

The fourth element of increasing your writing income is to get paid more by clients, publishers, and editors. Although this may seem like the most difficult of the four elements, in can in many cases be done.

Chapter 12. Where to Find (and How to Reach) Better Paying Markets

Instead of trying to squeeze more money out of modest paying sources, writers who want to make a lot of money should target the best-paying markets, clients, editors, and publishers. This chapter is designed to guide the reader to:

* book publishers that pay the biggest advances and highest royalties
* magazines that pay the biggest fees
* corporate clients and assignments that pay best
* other lucrative markets for writers (from greeting card companies to graphic designers producing annual reports)

Chapter 13. How to Negotiate Higher Fees, Advances, and Royalties

Chapter 13 is a comprehensive lesson in a topic covered in virtually every selling seminar but very few writing seminars: How to negotiate better fees and get paid more money. Readers will learn how and when to ask for more money, how to gain the best position for negotiating, when to back down and accept the offer, and when to pass. Writers will increase their fee per project 10 to 25% in a short time using these simple methods. Also covered in chapter 13: How to find and work with agents, reps, packagers, and others who can market and sell your services and negotiate deals for you.

Chapter 14. Secrets of the Super-Rich: What Does it Take to Make $100,000 a Year or More as a Writer?

The average writer in the United States earns around $25,000 annually. A few best-selling authors earn seven figure incomes, but there's no path that guarantees bestsellerdom. In between these extremes, there is a small and select group of freelancers who regularly earn six figure incomes equivalent to what doctors, airline pilots, attorneys, accountants, and professionals in other fields earn.

Chapter 14 discusses some of the interesting and innovative ways in which "nontraditional" writers earn lots of money. The text will include interviews with, and stories about, noncelebrity "superstar" writers earning $100,000 to $500,000 a year. Case histories include:

* a technical writer who makes $100,000 a year doing systems documentation
* a direct mail writer who makes $200,000 a year traveling the globe teaching businesspeople to market their products and services more effectively
* a former humor writer who earns $2,500 a day teaching business writing to corporate executives

* a freelance writer who has earned over $2 million writing about — and teaching others to be — better organized
* a writer who has become a self made millionaire self publishing his writings and selling them via mail.

Readers will see that the "writer starving in a garret" image is a self-created condition, not a marketplace necessity. Many writers earn handsome incomes allowing them and their families to enjoy comfortable upper-middle-class lives; a few even become rich.

In addition to practicing the four principles in this book — writing faster, writing more, selling more, charging more — many of these writers are successful because they work in nontraditional areas. The entrepreneurial or clever writer can break out of the $25,000 a year trap by taking advantage of a fifth principle: supply and demand.

The principle works as follows: When supply outweighs demands, pay scales are low. That's why most article and book writers don't earn much money. When demand outweighs supply, writers can charge a premium. That's why specialists doing work in areas most other writers have not discovered earn the big money. The chapter will close with guidelines on how to find little-known areas where there is brisk demand and minimal competition.

Appendix. Sources and Resources
Books, periodicals, directories, home pages, organizations, conferences, seminars, software, products (e.g., Day Timers), and other resources writers can use to increase their productivity and earnings.

# CHAPTER 6

# WRITING A POWERFUL BOOK PROPOSAL

If you are to have any chance of selling your book idea to a publishing house and becoming a published book author, it's absolutely essential to learn to write effective book proposals. You are asking a publisher to invest his time and money in your idea. Be sure you give him a strong and intelligently presented book proposal.

According to the American Society of Journalists and Authors: "A proposal is a detailed presentation of the book you want to write. It includes a description of the book, the likely market for it, a chapter by chapter outline, an author's bio, and a sample chapter or two."

This is easy if (a) you know the steps involved in writing such a proposal and know what information you need to include in your proposal, and (b) you have a sample book proposal in hand you can "copy" and use as a model in developing your own proposal.

This chapter fills both those needs. It teaches you step-by-step how to write a winning book proposal, and each section of explanation is followed by an excerpt from an actual book proposal.

The model I use is the proposal for my book, *How To Promote Your Own Business*, which was published by New American Library in 1983. It's not the best or the worst proposal I ever wrote, but it's a pretty good example of a solid proposal that sold quickly.

If you were to delete my instructions and paste the excerpts together, you'd have my proposal exactly as it was submitted to the publisher (except where I have indicated an omission).

To give you a model proposal in its entirety, I have included the proposal for a more recent book of mine, *Selling Your Services*, in Appendix D.

All proposals should be typed double-spaced on good-quality white paper. The pages should not be stapled; they should be held together with a large paper clip or binder clip ... or, you might put the pages in a folder.

Proposals should not be folded but should be mailed flat in a 9" X 12" envelope. I use folders or cardboard to protect the pages.

Every book proposal should contain these eight basic sections:

1. Title Page
2. Overview
3. Format
4. Market
5. Promotion
6. Competition
7. Author's Biography
8. Outline/Table of Contents (this is your content outline).

Now, not every author does it exactly the same. Some may combine sections, or have more sections than listed here, and you should feel free to adapt my method to your own needs, or take something good from someone else's proposal and put it in your own.

All I'm doing is showing you one method of writing proposals – a method that has proven effective time and time again.

Okay. Let's take a look at each section in detail:

# 1. TITLE PAGE

This is simple enough. Just type the words "Book proposal" at the top of the page. Then type the book title in the center of the page. Put the author's name (your name) underneath. In the lower right corner, type in your address, phone number, and the name and contact information for your agent (if you have one).

Here is the title page (condensed to save space) from my proposal for *How To Promote Your Own Business:*

**BOOK PROPOSAL**
*How To Promote Your Own Business*
by
Gary Blake and Robert W. Bly
174 Holland Avenue
New Milford, NJ 07646
(201) 385-1220
Agent: Dominick Abel, (212) 877-0710

# 2. OVERVIEW

Someone once said, "Every good idea can be written on the back of a business card." And that's the secret to writing a good overview.

Editors are busy people. Your proposal must immediately communicate the essence or key idea of your book to the editor. If the editor doesn't immediately understand (a) what your book is about, (b) who it is for, and (c) why people should want to buy it, she will probably send it back with a quick rejection.

The lead paragraph from the overview of the proposal for *How To Promote Your Own Business* does just that. It concisely describes what the book is (a promotion guide) and who it is for (entrepreneurs and business owners).

The rest of the overview expands on this description, summarizes the unique features of the book, and outlines the benefits the reader will get from reading the book:

*How To Promote Your Own Business*
by Robert W. Bly and Gary Blake

*How To Promote Your Own Business* is not a book for the professional publicist, promoter, or advertising man. Rather, it is a practical working guide for the 10.8 million Americans who own their own businesses, and the entrepreneurs who start 250,000 new businesses each year.

*How To Promote Your Own Business* uses a nonacademic approach. Every aspect of promoting the small to medium-size business is given the "how-to" treatment. Light, concise chapters tell readers what a given promotion is, what it can accomplish, and how much it will cost. Readers will learn how to create anything from a one-page flier or press release to a full-scale promotional campaign ... whether they do it themselves, or hire professional help.

There will be separate chapters on these topics:
* Promotional planning
* Sales literature
* Budgeting
* Print advertising
* Radio and TV advertising
* Copywriting
* Newsletters
* Production
* Displays
* Publicity
* Special promotions
* Direct mail and mail order
* Measuring results

Each of these chapters will have practical, easy-to-use hints and tips on how to do the promotion right — and at reasonable cost. Numerous charts, checklists, and promotional "do's and don'ts" will make it easy for the reader to progress through the book and use it as an instructional manual in producing his or her advertising, publicity, and sales promotion.

Real-life case histories will be blended into the text of each chapter. These case histories will show how specific businesses used a promotion to get their message across and increase sales. These examples will include a wide variety of businesses, from bookstores and bake shops, to home furnishings and handbags, to restaurants and real estate agents.

The entire book will be richly illustrated with samples of actual promotions including sales letters, fliers, ads, press releases, letterhead, radio commercial scripts, and TV commercial storyboards.

*[more description followed]*

*How To Promote Your Own Business* is unique because it goes right to the heart of the problem: How can the owner or manager of a small business — a person with little time, money, and promotion expertise — promote his business as effectively as his bigger, wealthier competitors?

## 3. FORMAT

The next section, format, tells the editor how lengthy the book will be and how it will be organized. It is here you tell the estimated word length, number of chapters, organization (for example, whether the book will be divided into major sections), special features (case histories, checklists, exercises), visuals (photos, diagrams, charts, illustrations), and so on.

Here is the format section from my proposal for *How To Promote Your Own Business:*

### FORMAT

*How To Promote Your Own Business* will run approximately 60,000 to 70,000 words in length. Among the graphics to be included are sample ads, fliers, press releases, radio spots, brochures, cover letters, coupons, solicitation letters, mailing lists, examples of various typefaces, catalogs, business cards, and letterhead.

Brief real-life case histories will be blended into the text. These case histories will show how owners of a variety of small businesses used promotions to increase their sales. The case histories, most of which the authors were directly involved with, will detail the circumstances, costs, options, and results of each promotion.

The book will have 18 chapters. Most of the chapters will contain numbered hints and tips which provide the reader with a step-by-step guide to estimating, implementing, and evaluating a variety of relatively low-cost promotions and promotional campaigns.

# 4. MARKET

"Market" is another word for audience. Who is the book written for? Who will buy it? Is this audience of sufficient size to justify publication of a book for them? These are the questions you must address in this section of the proposal.

Most books today deal with specialized topics and are aimed at audiences with special interests. Publishers do not have the time or staff to research these markets, and as a result, your proposal must demonstrate and prove that an audience for your book actually exists.

For example, let's say you wanted to write a guidebook on how to cope with infertility. Your proposal would have to convince the editor that there are enough infertile couples in the U.S. to justify publication of a book on this topic.

One way to do this would be to cite a statistic from a reliable source, such as an article in the New York Times or a report published by the American Medical Association. (As it happens, one out of five couples in the U.S. is infertile.)

Here's the marketing section from *How To Promote Your Own Business:*

MARKET

*How To Promote Your Own Business* reaches out to several strong, large markets:

1. Small business. The primary market for the book is the owner or manager of a small service, retail, wholesale, or manufacturing business. According to the U.S. Small Business Administration, there are 10.8 million

small businesses in the United States. One third of these are service businesses; one fourth, retail.

2. Entrepreneurs. Since 1976, nearly a million Americans have started their own businesses; 250,000 new small businesses are started each year. Nine out of ten of these ventures fail; successful promotion can significantly tip the odds in favor of success.

In addition to these new businesses, 3.5 million established companies change hands every year (according to an article in Forbes (11/21/81)). Therefore, 3.5 million new owners and managers will need information on how to promote their newly acquired businesses.

*[listings of more markets followed here]*

## 5. PROMOTION

Use the "Promotion" section of your proposal to give the editor any suggestions you have on how to sell, market, promote, and publicize your book.

You cannot realistically expect editors and publishers to be experts on all the topics covered by the books they publish. For this reason, they rely on authors who naturally have a greater knowledge of the audience they're writing to for help in marketing.

The more ways you can help the editor sell your book, the better.

For instance, let's say you submit a proposal on a book titled *How to Breed Snails for Fun and Profit*. An editor might wonder, "How can I reach all the snail enthusiasts who might be interested in buying this book?"

In the promotion section of your proposal, you mention that you are a member of the American Society of Snail Breeders, and as a member you can rent the membership mailing list at a discount, and that it contains the names and addresses of 120,000 snail hobbyists.

Suddenly, the editor sees a way to reach your audience, and you've removed one more obstacle in the way of the editor giving you a "yes" decision on your proposal.

Recently, a publisher said he "might" make an offer on a book I had been trying to sell, but was hesitant because he didn't know if there were any mailing lists available. Fortunately, in preparation for writing the book proposal, I had contacted a mailing list broker and obtained information on a number of promising mailing lists. Within minutes after I faxed this information to my agent and the publisher, he called her to say he wanted to go ahead with the contract.

However, keep in mind that most major publishing houses sell primarily through bookstores and to libraries. If your book can only be marketed through direct mail to a specialized list, the NY mainstream publishers will probably not be interested. Therefore, suggest a mailing, by all means, but only as a secondary or ancillary marketing tactic; never imply that it's the only way the book will sell or that it must be done for the book to succeed. (If such is the case, perhaps publishing with a major NY publishing house is not the best option for you; see chapter 12 on self-publishing.)

Here is the promotion section for *How To Promote Your Own Business:*

### PROMOTION

Promotion for this book shouldn't be difficult to obtain: Press releases could be sent to editors at the more than 200 business magazines nationwide, and to every business columnist in the United States. Releases should also go to management consultant organizations, as well as experts on the start-up of small businesses.

The direct mail possibilities for this book are almost endless because this book would have great relevance to organizations whose purpose it is to advance its members. Chambers of Commerce, professional women's groups, medical groups, and The American Management Association will want to share this book with their members.

*How To Promote Your Own Business* has wide potential for serialization. Among the best possibilities are *Venture,* Inc., *Entrepreneur, Black Enterprise,* and any of the dozen or so inflight magazines that regularly carry features pertaining to business.

For a variety of other promotional ideas...see *How To Pro-*

*mote Your Own Business.* It's a rich sourcebook of ideas on promoting unusual projects in unusual ways. And that's why this book has such broad appeal: It gives the average person the tool he or she needs to become independent, promote a business effectively, and bring in customers and clients.

Although I think most of the other sections of this proposal are pretty good, this section seems a bit weak to me now. What's missing are some promotional ideas unique to this book and its audience.

For example, you might suggest sending fliers on the book to the hundreds of local offices maintained by SCORE (Service Corps of Retired Executives), an organization that provides free consulting services to start-up businesses. Reason: A lot of entrepreneurs (translation: potential buyers for the book) walk into these offices each day looking for just this type of information.

Based on the material in *How to Promote Your Own Business* and other books we had written for entrepreneurs, my co-author and I decided to promote the books with a seminar on starting and running a small business. In one of the most ill-conceived book promotions of all time, we decided to hand out fliers advertising the seminar and book at the Port Authority and Penn Station in New York City during the morning rush hour.

We figured we would catch people at the precise time they were most disgruntled with work and open to the idea of starting their own business. The headline of the flier was, **"SICK AND TIRED OF COMMUTING?"**

We thought this would generate interest and enthusiasm; instead, it generated responses ranging from indifference and annoyance to outright hostility. Apparently, the commuters perceived that we were belittling them. One grabbed the flier, which was on heavy paper, crumpled it, and shoved it into my face, scratching my eye. So although you should be creative in promotion, be aware that not every creative promotion works.

## 6. COMPETITION

You've explained to the editor what your book is about, who it's written for, and why these people need it.

Now the editor asks, "Yes, but aren't there many other books on the market that cover this topic? And if so, why should we publish yours?"

The "Competition" section of your proposal answers this question.

If there are no books that directly compete with yours, the competition section says so and gives some evidence that your answer is based on research, not just your own belief.

If there are books with similar titles to yours... or that attempt to cover the same ground...you have to identify these books and demonstrate how yours is different and better (how to do this is discussed in detail in chapter 4).

Here is the competition section for *How To Promote Your Own Business:*

### COMPETITION

*BOOKS IN PRINT* lists approximately 200 books on small businesses and hundreds more on advertising, public relations, publicity, and sales promotion. However, there are only five books that deal with advertising or promotion for small business. None of these five is published in hardcover by a major trade publisher. The books are:

1. *How To Advertise And Promote Your Small Business* by Connie McClung Siegel, John Wiley & Sons, Inc., 1978, 128 pages, $4.95 trade paperback.

This book is part of John Wiley's "Small Business Series." The author neglects several vital areas of small business promotion including mail order, sales literature, trade shows and displays, contests, and newsletters. There are very few examples of actual promotions, and the author gives no indication of the costs involved. The book does not provide step-by-step instructions for selecting and executing promotions.

2. *The Successful Promoter: 100 Surefire Ideas For Selling Yourself, Your Product, Your Organization* by Ted

Schwarz, Contemporary Books, Inc., 1976, 223 pages, $4.95, trade paperback.

This book, like Siegel's, gives no indication of what a promotion costs to execute. There are no photographs or illustrations, so the reader cannot see what a successful ad, flier, or mailer looks like. It would be difficult to use the book as a working promotion guide since the long chapters (average length: 8,000 words) are not broken up into numbered step-by-step instructions or even short, readable sections. Further, there is no chapter on what may be the most important area of promotion: sales literature.

[descriptions of the other 3 competing books followed]

## 7. AUTHOR'S BIOGRAPHY

Now that you have told the editor why your book is unique and why it is needed, her next question may be, "Okay, I like the book...but why are *you* the best person to write it?"

The fact that the book is your idea and that you brought the proposal to the editor is not enough to get her to buy it. Often, an editor will receive many proposals at one time for books on the same topic! If they all offer a similar approach, the author's credentials may play a big role in which proposal she buys.

The "About the Author" section should focus on three aspects of your background:

(1) Any expertise or credentials you have in the subject matter your book deals with,

(2) your previous publishing credits, and

(3) any experience you have in promoting books (for example, whether you've been interviewed on radio and TV shows before).

Here is the "About the Authors" section from our *How To Promote Your Own Business* proposal:

ABOUT THE AUTHORS

GARY BLAKE is the author of *The Status Book* (Doubleday), which was syndicated by The Los Angeles Times Syndicate and excerpted in Book Digest. He has appeared on more than 50 radio and TV talk shows in New York, Chicago, and Boston.

Mr. Blake's work has appeared in The New York Times Book Review, The Washington Post, Harper's, Travel & Leisure, Family Circle, Advertising Age, and Glamour. He is director of The Communication Workshop, a publicity and sales promotion company. He has designed and implemented promotional programs for a variety of small businesses in food, health and beauty, apparel, retail, direct mail, publishing, real estate, medicine, finance, entertainment, and other industries.

ROBERT W. BLY is a freelance copywriter specializing in industrial advertising. He has written and produced ads, brochures, catalogs, direct mail, press releases, AV presentations, and trade show exhibits for companies in data processing, defense, electronics, chemical equipment, telecommunications, and related industries. Mr. Bly was advertising manager for Koch Engineering Company and a staff writer for Westinghouse. For the past year, he has taught seminars in "How to Promote Your Own Business" for Westwinds in New York City.

Together, Gary Blake and Robert W. Bly have written *Technical Writing: Structure, Standards, And Style,* which the McGraw-Hill Book Company will publish in 1982.

## 8. CONTENT OUTLINE

You have given your editor an overview of the concept of your book. But that is not enough. Now you must show in detail how you plan to fill the 200 pages and deliver the 70,000 to 80,000 words you are asking her to buy from you.

Remember the content outline you created in chapter 5? All you have to do now is insert it into your proposal here.

Content outlines can be in paragraph form, bullets, or a combination.

A content outline written in narrative form gives, in a few paragraphs per chapter, brief descriptions of the purpose and overall content of each chapter. A content outline in narrative format for my forthcoming Writer's Digest Book, *How to Make $50,000+ A Year Writing* is reprinted in chapter 5.

A content outline written in bullet form presents a list of the specific topics covered in each chapter. This was the format we used in our proposal for *How To Promote Your Own Business.* Here is a section of that content outline:

Table of Contents

Introduction: How This Book Can Help You Bring in Business and Increase Profits

CHAPTER 1: WHAT PROMOTION IS ALL ABOUT

* Why promote your business?
* The four types of promotion
  -personal selling
  -advertising
  -publicity
  -sales promotion
* What promotion will work best for YOUR business? (in this section will include a list of all the types of small businesses and the promotions they can use)

CHAPTER 2: PLANNING YOUR PROMOTIONS

* Writing a business plan
* Target marketing: Define your customers...
  -by geographic location
  -by age, income, sex, and other demographics
  -by business and job title
* Questions to ask when planning promotions:
  -How can I reach my prospects?
  -What do I want to say to them?
  -What is the best way to say it?
  -How do I want them to respond?

CHAPTER 3: HOW TO BUDGET PROMOTIONS

The methods of budgeting include:
-Percentage of sales
-Match the competition
-Historical — The "This is what we've always done" approach
-Whatever you can afford
-"Task-to-objective" - Spend what it takes to achieve your planned goals
[descriptions of remaining chapters followed]

The content outline is usually the final section of the book proposal, although your proposal might contain two more sections in addition to the eight listed:

9. Supplementary materials

10. Sample chapters.

## 9.  SUPPLEMENTARY MATERIAL.

You can add appendices at the end of your proposal to help strengthen your case, make your proposal more attractive, and convince the publisher they should publish your book.

Here are some typical proposal supplements authors have used to sell their books:

1. If you have had other books published and reviewed favorably in the press, attach a typed list of excerpts from these reviews at the end of your proposal. Editors are made comfortable by the fact that your previous books have been well-received.

2. If you have achieved some status as a celebrity or expert in the field your book deals with, photocopy some of your press clippings and attach them to the end of your proposal. This has the same effect as #1 above.

3. If you have written an article on the same subject as your book (or one of its chapters), attach this at the end of the proposal as an example of your writing style (and to stress the fact that you have been published).

4. If you feel the editor may be unaware of the importance or popularity of your subject matter, attach article reprints and press clippings that show recent media coverage of your topic (even if these are not written by or about you).

One author I know of wrote a proposal for a book on aerobic exercise when aerobics was just on the verge of becoming hot — and his attaching recent articles on the popularity of aerobics helped sell the book to his editor.

In addition to the supplemental material, your editor may also request sample chapters.

## 10. SAMPLE CHAPTERS

I have sold many books just on the strength of my proposal. But in several instances – especially early in my career, before I had established a track record – the proposal by itself did not close the sale. "Send us a sample chapter or two," editors said, "then we can make a decision about whether to publish your book or not."

Should you do it?

If an editor likes your proposal enough to be interested, but is not convinced either that the book is exactly what she wants or that you have the ability to write it, she may ask you to write and submit one or two sample chapters "on spec," meaning you write and submit them with no commitment or payment from the publisher unless they like the samples and make you an offer on the book.

While I am not a big fan of spec work, if a legitimate publisher shows enough interest to request sample chapters, you probably should write them. To refuse such a request would almost surely end the editor's interest in working with you; it's a snub.

On the other hand, if you write the sample chapters and the editor does not buy, you have a stronger package to show other publishing houses. And if the book doesn't sell, you can always publish these chapters as articles or booklets. So the down-side is minimal.

Which chapters should you submit as samples? Write chapter one and then whatever chapter you feel would be your strongest chapter. The strong chapter shows your book at its best, while chapter one gives the editor a feel for how you'd start and "get into" the meat of your book.

### ADDITIONAL TIPS ON ADDING SELLING POWER TO YOUR PROPOSAL

If you have access to special information, research material, or other "inside information" other authors do not have, mention this either in your overview or in the format section. Some editors like to see proof that the authors know where to get the necessary information and research material once they have the go-ahead to write the book. Show that you know your subject — or that you know where to go to find out more about it.

Use numbers, figures, and statistics. For example, instead of saying, "There are certainly a lot of people who hate their boss and would buy a book on *How To Work For A Jerk*," say, "According to a recent article in Psychology Today, 75% of workers surveyed said they 'hated' or 'disliked' their immediate supervisor." Specifics are more credible than generalities and show that you have done your homework.

Writing a good book proposal is an essential step toward your goal of selling your book and becoming a published book author. When you sit down to write your book proposal, organize your material into the sections I've outlined. Read the excerpts from my sample proposal a few times to get a feel for the style. Then follow what I've done or adjust the format to meet your own needs.

Try not to get too worried about format. It's helpful to study the proposals done by other authors (especially those proposals that sold), but use them as a guide only. Remember, there's no "official" proposal format, no "right" and "wrong" way carved in stone.

Rather, put yourself in the editor's shoes. Or the literary agent's. What does she want?

(1) She wants to buy books on interesting topics that will appeal to book buyers (or a certain segment of book buyers). The book must offer enough information, how-to advice, or entertainment value to motivate the reader to pay $9.95 or $14.95 or $19.95 for it.

(2) She wants a book that is either unique or, if it's not unique, is somewhat different from (and better than) other books on the subject — or else why would anyone want to read it?

(3) She wants to be sure that there really is a book in your idea. In other words, do you have enough material to fill 200

pages? What will you fill those pages with? How will the material be organized?

(4) Finally, she wants to be convinced that you are qualified to write it, that you can write it, and that you'll do a good job (write a good book, meet your deadline, and not be difficult to work with).

After you've completed your proposal, read what you have written. Does it make you want to buy the book? If not, go back to the word processor until the material is much stronger.

Make your proposal the best it can be — this gives you the best chance of selling your idea to a publisher.

■ ■ ■ ■ ■ ■ ■ ■ ■ ■

***EXERCISE:*** Pick one of the book ideas you came up with earlier. I recommend you pick the one that has the most appeal to you and has also passed the 5-question checklist evaluation process, which indicates the book might also appeal to a publisher.

Write the "Overview" section for a proposal on this book. Put it aside and read it later. Now go back and make it stronger.

If you are satisfied with this overview and feel strongly that you want to pursue this book idea, go ahead and write the rest of the proposal.

Once you have a complete proposal, go on to the next chapter — and the next step in the 8-step book selling and marketing process.

If, after reading your overview, you do not feel enthusiastic about the book, pick another idea from your book idea list and repeat this exercise. Do it until you have written a complete proposal for a book you feel enthusiastic and passionate about.

Then go on to the next step and chapter.

# CHAPTER 7

# GETTING A LITERARY AGENT TO REPRESENT YOU

While it is possible to sell your book to a publishing house without the help of a literary agent, having an agent represent you will greatly increase the odds of success.

"Publishers decided years ago that it was uneconomical for them to read unsolicited manuscripts," says Arthur M. Klebanoff, president, Scott Meredith Literary Agency. "Publishers rely on agents for recommendations."

That being the case, I recommend you initially concentrate on selling yourself and your book idea to an agent.

If you can convince a good agent to take on the project, then the agent will have primary responsibility for selling the book, saving you time, and increasing your chances of acceptance.

If you cannot get an agent to represent you, then you can represent the book yourself and try to sell it on your own (this is covered in chapter 8).

I've done it both ways, and based both on personal experience and the state of the publishing industry today, my advice is to get an agent, if you can.

The exception might be if you have a pre-existing relationship with a book publisher (or know someone who does) and feel your book is exactly right for that particular publisher.

Okay. Let's get right to your questions.

*Q: "Why do I need an agent? Can't I sell the book myself?"*

A: You should try to get an agent because most editors today will not read your material unless it is submitted by an agent.

Agents act as "screening devices" for editors. Although submission by an agent does not guarantee a sale (far from it), the editor will at least look at the material. The editor's logic in doing so is that if the agent thinks the book is good enough to represent, it is at least worth taking a look at.

With an agent, your book goes directly to the editor. When you submit the book yourself, without an agent, it will probably go to a "slush pile" — a room filled with unsolicited and unagented materials from unknown authors. Here, it will be screened by several people, who have the power to reject it before it ever gets to a real editor. It might first be read by an outside "reader" (person hired to evaluate book proposals), and then by a junior editor on staff, before it has a chance to get to a "real" editor (the odds of your proposal making it all this way are slim at best).

I know that this is so, based on my own experience as a "reader" for a major publishing house. On a freelance basis, I was hired to read and evaluate book proposals. On average, I recommended perhaps only one in ten (or even fewer) for publication.

Having your material start at this lower level of approval dramatically reduces the odds of acceptance, because each "screener" is likely to reject the overwhelming majority of material. So you can see why having an agent gives you a better chance of making the sale.

As a rule of thumb, the larger the publishing house, the more vital it is to have an agent. The smaller the publishing house, the more likely they are to look at unsolicited proposals not represented by an agent.

### Q: "Any Other Reasons To Have An Agent?"

A: In addition to increasing your chances of making a sale, an agent can keep up with the publishing industry and know which publishers and editors would be most enthusiastic about your book. This translates (theoretically) into greater chances for a sale, higher advances, and better promotion for your book.

Another area where agents help is in negotiating favorable book contracts for authors. A book contract has numerous clauses in fine print, each of which is negotiable and can greatly affect your total income from the book.

Authors, being nervous about upsetting the publisher, are unlikely to push for more favorable terms. Agents, on the other hand, are expected to do so, and *can* do so without damaging the author-editor relationship.

### Q: "What Does An Agent Do?"

A: A literary agent acts as your representative, aggressively selling your book ideas, proposals, and manuscripts to publishing houses.

The basic function of an agent is sales. A good agent is one who is able to sell your writing and get you the best deal in terms of advance, royalty, publisher, promotional budget, and quality of editor and publisher.

### Q: "How Do Agents Get Paid?"

A: An agent collects a percentage of all advances, royalties, and other income (e.g., sale of serial rights, movie rights, etc.) generated by your book. Typically, this compensation ranges from 10 to 15 percent.

In most contracts, there is a clause specifying that the advance and royalty checks go first to the agent, who deducts his or her commission and then sends you a check for the money owed you. You need not worry about this clause. The agent will add it for your approval and signature.

### Q: "Do I Pay The Agent To Market My Manuscript?"

A: You do not pay any fees to your agent until he or she makes a sale for you, at which time the agent receives a commission as discussed above.

Agents typically absorb phone expenses, postage, travel, lunches with editors, and other expenses involved in marketing your book and running their agency. However, it is traditional for the author to pay for the cost of photocopying book manuscripts and provide the agent with as many copies as required (usually 3 or 4 for simultaneous submissions to multiple publishers).

### Q: *"What About Agents Who Charge 'Reading Fees' Or Ask For Other Payments?"*

A: Some agents do charge to read and critique manuscripts, but such services are often worthless.

Most legitimate agents, if interested in your idea, will review your material and immediately tell you whether they're interested in representing you, without charging an up-front fee.

By the same token, since they are not yet on your "payroll," these agents will not spend a lot of time with you over the phone or provide you with a lengthy critique or editing of your manuscript. So if you want critique or editing services, you can always hire people in that business. (Many advertise in Writer's Digest, and some of the people in Appendix K can perform these services for you).

There are some legitimate agents who, if uncertain about your idea or your qualifications, will agree to review the proposal or manuscript for a fee. Many will refund the fee if they go on to represent and sell the book for you.

### Q: *"How Involved Do Agents Get With Their Authors?"*

A: The agent's role is primarily that of sales agent, not editorial assistant, writing partner, or hand-holder. As the author, *you* must come up with the ideas, write the proposals and sample chapters, and – once the agent makes the sale – write the book.

Some agents go beyond the role of business agent. Some are hand-holders, acting as part-psychologist, part-cheerleader to support their author's "artistic temperament" in times of crisis, depression, or "writer's block."

Some agents, by choice, get very involved in formulating ideas and structuring book proposals. This is a nice extra. But it is not part of the standard service.

One thing you *should* expect from your agent, however, is

a frank, honest, and specific evaluation of your ideas and book proposals. If the agent doesn't like an idea, he should be able to say *why* he thinks it will not sell — and perhaps suggest another angle that will turn the book into a winner.

By the same token, if he thinks your idea is good but your proposal is weak and will not sell it, he should tell you so — and then provide specific suggestions on how you can improve your proposal so it becomes the marketing tool he needs to get a publisher to buy the book.

### Q: "How Do I Go About Finding An Agent?"

A: The best place to start is with your own personal contacts. If you don't know someone who has published a book, chances are a friend of a friend, or a relative of a friend, may know someone. Ask that author for a referral. Does he have an agent he can recommend to you? Does he have any suggestions on which agents to contact?

### Q: "What If I Don't Know Anyone In Publishing?"

A: Here's a technique that has worked well for me.

Go to a bookstore or library and look at recent books on topics similar to the book you want to write. Now, read the acknowledgments at the beginning of the book. Many authors will thank their literary agents by name in the acknowledgments. Write down the names of these agents, look them up in a directory such as *Writer's Digest* or *Literary Marketplace* and contact them (appendix B lists agents and also provides resources for obtaining the names of agents not on my list).

This technique of looking for agents in book acknowledgments works well because agents, like other people, have their own particular interests, and an agent will be more receptive to your idea if it fits in with the type of books she likes to work with.

### Q: "What's The Best Way To Contact An Agent?"

A: Send a brief letter of introduction. Explain where you got their name, who you are, and briefly describe the type of book you want to write. If you have writing credentials or are an established expert in the subject matter of your proposed book, say so.

Close your letter by offering to send the agent a book proposal, outline, or other background material that describes your proposed book in more detail. A typical letter might read as follows:

---

Mr. Joe Jones
Jones Literary Agency
Anytown, USA

Dear Mr. Jones:

I notice that you are the agent for *How To Raise Poodles For Fun And Profit* by Sue Smith. Would you consider looking at a proposal for a poodle book that focuses on health, obedience, and grooming?

For 9 years I have been the owner of OODLES OF POODLES, a boutique specializing in poodle care. We do haircuts, styling, bathing, nail trimming, bathing, and poodle "charm school," and can offer poodle owners a lot of valuable how-to advice on these subjects.

Would you be interested in seeing a proposal for a nonfiction do-it-yourself book on taking care of pet poodles? I can have the material on your desk within a few days.

A self-addressed stamped envelope is enclosed. Thanks for your consideration,

Sincerely,

Dirk Johnson, Owner
Oodles of Poodles

P.S. Poodles owned by our clients have won 15 "Best of Show" blue ribbons at dog shows in our state since 1990.

### Q: "What If The Agent Doesn't Respond?"

A: Agents are busy people and are flooded with letters of this type. Be prepared to wait at least 2 to 6 weeks. If you haven't heard anything after that time, send a follow-up letter.

Do not be rude, sarcastic, or angry in your follow-up. Be polite. Ask if the agent received your original letter. If not, briefly describe your book and offer to send your book proposal if the agent would like to see it.

### Q: "Should I Telephone The Agent If I Still Have Not Heard Anything?"

A: It depends. If you are professional and mature in your dealings, a brief phone call is fine. But if you are going to lose your temper or rant and rave, stick to letter writing. Agents do not want to deal with authors who are pests.

### Q: "Is It Okay To Send My Letter To More Than One Agent At A Time?"

A: Yes, although if your material is really good, and you have a strong reason to expect a favorable reaction from a particular agent (e.g., the agent and you were introduced by a mutual friend), then you make more of an impression offering it to that agent first on an exclusive basis.

### Q: "What Should I Look For In An Agent?"

A: Track record is the key factor. What books has the agent sold? What authors does the agent represent? To what publishers has the agent sold these books? What kind of advances did the agent get for the authors?

According to Bonita Nelson, of the B.K. Nelson Literary Agency, qualities of a good agent include:

➤ selling ability
➤ contacts and relationships
➤ enthusiasm

➤ communication
➤ knowledge of the changing market
➤ ability to evaluate book ideas
➤ negotiation skills.

### Q: "What Happens If The Agent Likes My Book Idea?"

A: He or she will probably ask to see a book proposal (if it's a nonfiction book) or a chapter outline and some sample chapters (if it's a novel).

If the agent is favorably impressed by the proposal, outline, and sample chapters, he or she will ask you to sign an "agent's agreement" and congratulations – you have a literary agent!

### Q: "Should I Have My Lawyer Check The Agent's Agreement?"

A: Although these agreements are usually simple, it's not a bad idea to have an attorney look over any important document you sign.

The agreement is usually in the form of an informal written agreement between agent and author. It says that the agent will represent you and spells out the terms of compensation (in other words, the percentage of the book income paid to the agent.)

The agreement will also state that you are to handle all your dealings with publishers through the agent and not sell any books on your own or through other agents.

Make sure the agreement has a clause that says either of you can cancel it at any time with a 30 or 60 day notice. You want to be able to end the relationship without obligation if the agent is not performing to your satisfaction.

### Q: "What If The Agent Doesn't Sell My Book?"

A: It does happen, but it indicates that either the agent used poor judgment in accepting your book to sell or the agent is not good at selling. A good agent can probably sell 80 percent of the books that he accepts from his authors. One missed sale is acceptable. Two failures in a row may mean it's time to re-evaluate the relationship.

How much time should you give your agent to sell your book? Publishers move slowly, so it may be many months before the agent gets an answer from each publisher he submits to. However, if he doesn't sell the book within 6 to 12 months, chances are he probably never will. Prolific how-to author Jeffrey Davidson says that if the book is rejected by the first ten publishers to review the proposal, the chances of making a sale become slim at best.

### Q: "What If I Don't Like The Deal My Agent Got For Me?"

A: Don't be so greedy. Most new authors have unrealistic expectations. An advance of $6,000 to $12,000 is quite acceptable for a first book...or a second...or a third — unless your title is a potential best-seller (or you are a celebrity).

If you are getting much less than a $3,000 to $5,000 advance per book, you may want to take some of your proposals or manuscripts to other agents (or show them to editors you know) to get a second opinion.

### Q: "What Happens If I Bring A New Book To My Agent And He Doesn't Like It?"

A: It can happen that an agent refuses to represent a book for a client because he thinks the book is not marketable.

If this happens more than once, you should rethink your relationship with your agent. Either she has lost interest and become indifferent to you, or you and she are no longer on the same wavelength when it comes to the projects you want to pursue. Whichever it is, you may want to start shopping for a new agent. Before you do, however, take another look at your idea. Perhaps the agent is right, and it does not have the commercial potential you originally thought. Ask the agent if there's an angle you can take to make it more salable.

Your author/agent agreement should specify that if your agent refuses to represent a particular book idea, you are then free to market it, either yourself or through another agent.

**Q:** *"What Happens If A Publisher Approaches Me About A Book Deal And I Think I Can Negotiate It Without My Agent's Help?"*

A: Don't do it. Fair play and good business dictate that all deals be directed through your agent. True, the agent will take his 10 to 15 percent share of the profits. But remember, agents do more than just make sales; they also negotiate favorable deals. A good agent is worth his 10 or 15 percent even when negotiating a deal that he didn't have to sell.

And if you have an agent, you should never, never talk money with a publisher. If an editor asks how much advance you would want to do a book, the answer is, "I'll have my agent call you." And then do precisely that.

# CHAPTER 8

# SELLING YOUR BOOK TO A PUBLISHING HOUSE

You've written a book proposal. Now you've got to sell it. How to go about that depends on whether you're doing it yourself or have convinced a literary agent to represent you.

As I said earlier, my recommendation is that you first try to get an agent who can do the selling for you. If that doesn't work, then you can try to sell it on your own, but your chances for a sale will be somewhat diminished. Yes, I've done it both with and without an agent. But I believe having a literary agent dramatically increases the odds of success.

## SELLING WITH A LITERARY AGENT

Your agent can approach the sale in a variety of ways, but the most common is to send your proposal simultaneously to multiple publishing houses. This is called a simultaneous or multiple submission.

The agent typically sends the book to between two and five publishers at one time. Which publishers are offered the book depends on (a) the agent's knowledge of the types of books these companies like, (b) the publisher's track record in successfully selling lots of copies of books like yours, (c) the personal preferences and interests of a particular editor at the house, (d) the agent's relationship with that particular editor, and (e) the advances, royalties, and contracts the publisher can offer.

Your agent will make phone calls first. Then, if there is any initial interest, he or she will send the proposal to those publishers. This is called a multiple submission, because the book is being submitted to multiple publishers simultaneously.

A variation of the multiple submission is the auction, where multiple publishers bid against one another to acquire the book. Auctions are usually held only when the book is predicted to be a big-seller and therefore highly desirable to the publishers. The agent names a dollar figure which is the minimum bid he or she will accept.

An exclusive submission means the agent submits the book initially to one publisher only and allows them to consider it with the promise it will not be offered to any other publishers for a specified period of time. Exclusive submissions are made when the agent feels a particular publisher would be "right" for the book and the publisher has indicated strong initial interest.

Publishers are slow to move, and your book may sit on someone's desk for 4 to 6 weeks before any action is taken or response is made. Some authors have waited for over a year to get a decision from a publishing house. But a professional agent usually can get a faster response.

Do not pester your agent by calling every other day to find out what is going on with your book. If the agent has news, he or she will tell you. Some agents like to be in frequent contact with clients; others only call when necessary. If your agent leans toward the latter, stay out of her way and let her do her job. Agents frown on pesky clients.

When an agent sells a book for me, I always acknowledge this in the acknowledgment section of the book. Since I write a lot of books, I send my agent a nice Christmas gift every year. When I started out, I gave a gift after every book sale, but this became expensive and overwhelming as my quantity went into the dozens.

## How The Publisher Makes The Decision

If the editor likes your book and wants to publish it, she will have to get approval from a committee before she can go ahead and make you an offer. This committee includes an "editorial board" (a group of senior editors), the editor-in-chief or publisher, and the sales and marketing departments.

The editorial board judges the book on its literary merit and looks primarily at whether the book will be interesting, have strong reader appeal, is amusing or entertaining, or is an important work that deserves publication.

The sales and marketing staff will do an analysis and vote for or against your book based on their estimate (an educated guess) of how many copies they think they can sell and how much revenue the book will bring in.

At most publishing houses the offer is not firm until approved by the editor-in-chief or publisher. These "head honchos" usually go with the decision of their editors and marketing and sales staff, but not always.

A positive initial response from an editor should not be taken to mean that you have made a sale. Far from it. Getting an editor who supports your book is the first step, but only a step. The editor must be able to sell your book to the committee, and if she can't, you won't get an offer.

Numerous times an editor has told my agent, "I like this book," and then come back to say, "I'm sorry, but I couldn't sell it to my committee." It's natural to be thrilled when an agent and then an editor are enthusiastic about your book. But don't get too excited. Until you have a contract in hand, you haven't made the sale.

If the editor or editorial committee decides against making you an offer, they will notify your agent by mail or phone. At this point the agent will probably take the book to another publishing firm for consideration.

If the publisher wants to publish your book, they will inform the agent, usually by phone. The agent and the publisher will then discuss terms and begin negotiations that will culminate in a firm offer and signed contract.

## SELLING YOUR BOOK ON YOUR OWN
## DIRECTLY TO A PUBLISHER

Much of what I've just described about selling with an agent applies to selling on your own. As an author representing yourself, however, you will probably be unable to get publishers to participate in an auction, and so you will either go the route of exclusive or multiple submissions.

Do an exclusive submission when you have some kind of "in" with a particular editor at a particular publishing house (e.g., you were introduced by a friend, met the editor at a writer's conference, etc.). If you do not have a relationship or "in" with any editors, then a multiple submission is best.

Here are some guidelines to help you sell your book on your own, directly to publishers:

➤ Get to know the market. Read *Writer's Market, Literary Marketplace (LMP), Publisher's Weekly,* and *Writer's Digest.* Pay attention to listings of various book publishers. Clip or photocopy listings of those who seem good candidates for your book, and keep a file of them.

Ask friends with contacts in the publishing industry for the names of editors and publishers who might be interested in your book. Browse libraries and bookstores for books in your category (e.g., business, computers, popular science, cookbooks), and take notes on which publishing companies publish these types of books.

Do all these things, and you can quickly compile a list of half a dozen or more publishers who are good candidates to publish your book. Appendix A lists some of the major publishers.

➤ Deal with a person, not a company. Call the publishers or check directories such as *Writer's Market* and *LMP* so that you can get the names of editors at these publishing companies. Always address correspondence to a specific editor by name, not generic title (e.g., "editor" or "for the editorial department"). Not sending material to a specific person guarantees your letter or proposal will go to the slush pile.

➤ Make the initial contact brief and to the point. A quick phone call or short note describing your book in a paragraph or two is the best way to make initial contact. Close by offering to send a proposal, if the editor wants to see one.

As a rule, a phone call works best if you have a relationship with the editor or were referred to him or her by a mutual colleague or acquaintance. If you are contacting the editor based on finding his or her name in a book or directory, a short letter is best.

➤ Follow-up. If you don't get a reply to your letter within 4 weeks, send a follow-up note or call the editor to ask whether your letter was received. If not, or if she doesn't remember it, state the title of your book, give a 30-second overview of your idea, and ask if the editor would like you to send a more detailed outline and proposal.

➤ Get a referral. Network. Ask friends, or friends of friends, or relatives, or people you meet at writer's conferences if they know any editors at the big publishing houses — and, if they do, can you contact that editor and use the person's name as a reference? An editor will be far more likely to treat you seriously if you are referred to them by somebody they know and respect, such as one of their authors.

➤ Act professionally. Publishers are inundated with letters, proposals, manuscripts, and phone calls from people whom they think of as "kooks" — wanna-be authors who will do or say anything to get their book published, and who cannot handle rejection, criticism, or suggestions in a positive and rational manner.

Even though *you* are not a kook, to many editors you are guilty until proven innocent. So, beginning with your initial contact and continuing through the entire selling process, all your communications with editors must be professional, direct, brief, and reasonable. Listen more than you talk. Be dignified and reserved. Avoid appearing artsy or idiosyncratic. Say what you have to say once, then stop.

Don't argue. Don't go on and on.

Act like a business professional, and you will get professional results. Act like one of the kooks, and you'll be treated accordingly.

➤ Be persistent. How To Get Your Book Published is much more important to you than it is to editors and their publishers. Therefore, you must take the initiative.

This means if one publisher rejects you, you make some calls and send your proposal to three other publishing companies. It means that if a dozen publishers have rejected your proposal, you don't give up; you see whether it could be improved or perhaps should be set aside and another idea tried.

Many would-be authors never get published simply because they aren't persistent and give up too early.

For instance, I tried to sell a book on comic book trivia in 1979 but got no takers. Instead of giving up, I put the proposal aside; worked on other projects; had many books published.

In 1993, I found an agent interested in my trivia book; redid the proposal; gave it to her. She sold it to Carol Publishing, and the book, *Comic Book Heroes*, was published in 1996.

➤ Be able to take rejection. You will probably get many rejections before you finally get a publisher to say yes. Expect this. Don't tell me "I took my book to five publishers and it didn't sell." You may have to try ten publishers or even more before one says "go."

*It's okay to feel bad about rejection, but it's not okay to let the negative opinion of a few editors derail your dream. Stephen King wrote three novels he couldn't sell before Doubleday bought Carrie. Sam Sinclair Baker had 17 publishers reject his Scarsdale Diet. The 18th bought it for a small advance, then it promptly went on to sell millions of copies and make Sam rich.*

Don't be overly sensitive to criticism. The authors who are already published did not need to have every editor at every publishing house love their book. They only needed one to say "Yes." That's all you need, too.

➤ Be open-minded. While you shouldn't give up because of some rejections or negative reviews of your material, do be open-minded. If half a dozen editors all say the same thing about your book (e.g., "you need to add a chapter on topic X"), the suggestion may be valid and should at least be considered by you.

It's a paradox: Writing is a solitary act performed by one person alone in a room sitting at a desk. But the product of writing is collaborative — virtually every published piece of writing (with the exception of many self-published materials) has been edited by someone other than the author. So don't resist editing; embrace it.

My friends who self publish say one of the advantages of self-publishing is they control the content of the book and do not have an editor interfering with their brilliant prose. To me, regular publishing is better, in that I get the input and guidance of a skilled book editor without paying a freelance editor a fee to do the work. Yes, sometimes I don't agree with the editor's comments. But they help far more often than they hurt.

➤ Ask for referrals. When a publisher turns you down, don't get mad and walk away. Instead, ask, "Do you have any colleagues you think this book might be right for?" Often they will refer you to editors at other publishing houses. When you contact those editors, you can say you were referred by the original editor, which will gain you more serious attention.

The same thing, incidentally, can work with agents. If an agent turns you down, ask if they have a colleague who might be interested in taking a look at your book. More than half the time, they will give you referrals to at least one or two other agents they know. Then you can contact these agents and say "so-and-so gave me your name."

## A BUYER'S MARKET

My view of book publishing is that it is a buyer's market. In terms of supply and demand, publishers are offered by authors many more books than they can publish, and therefore are able to pick and choose. On the other hand, most authors do not have many more publishers begging them for books than they can write for. As best-selling computer book author Roger C. Parker observes, "The traditional model for author/publisher relations is based on authors playing a subordinate role."

Keep in mind that it's probably more important to you that you get your book published than it is to any editor to buy it. If this frustrates you unduly, see chapter 12 on the pros and cons of self-publishing vs. traditional publishing. For myself, I have learned to live with it and continue to sell my books to mainstream publishing houses. Do what works best for you.

■ ■ ■ ■ ■ ■ ■ ■ ■ ■

*EXERCISE:* Using the resources in Appendices A and B, contact at least two dozen agents and publishers and present your book idea to them.

It will take several contacts before you feel comfortable and hone your approach.

Your goal is to get at least half a dozen or so agents and publishers to agree to look at your proposal. This should result either in having an agent take you on as a client or at least one offer from a major publishing company.

# CHAPTER 9

# NEGOTIATING AND SIGNING THE BOOK CONTRACT

Congratulations! You've gotten through the difficult part ... and now have an offer from a publisher who wants to publish your book.

You're probably excited, and you should be. This is a major accomplishment many people want to achieve but don't. You are going to be a published author, with all of the kudos, prestige, and fame that go with it.

But you are not quite there yet. You have to write the book. And even before that, you have to negotiate terms and fees with the publisher. These include:

➤ Your advance

➤ Hardcover royalties

➤ Paperback royalties

➤ First and second serializations

➤ Dramatization and audiovisual rights

➤ License to book clubs

➤ Translations and foreign editions

➤ Manuscript preparation, delivery, author's warranty

➤ Option

➤ Termination

➤ Author's copies and discount.

Let's define each term and see what it is reasonable for you to expect.

➤ **ADVANCES:** Advances are just that — money advanced against future royalties. Here's how it works:

Let's say you get a $10,000 advance and a royalty of $1 per book. On the first 10,000 books sold, the publisher gets all the money to cover the advance they paid you. When book number 10,001 is sold, you get a $1 royalty — and $1 for all books sold after that. Royalties are generally paid every 6 months.

What kind of advance can you, as a first-time author, expect?

According to the *National Writer's Union Guide To Freelance Rates & Standard Practices* (Cincinnati, Ohio: Writer's Digest Books, 1995), the average advance is $20,560 for a hardcover nonfiction book and $11,730 for a trade paperback nonfiction book. For a children's book, it's around $5,000. Authors of textbooks and professional reference books generally get advances in the $2,500 to $5,000 range.

Michael Larsen, a literary agent and author of *How to Find and Work With a Literary Agent* (Cincinnati, Ohio: Writer's Digest Books), says the advance for a nonfiction book will range from $5,000 to $15,000, with $7,500 being about average. I think his figures are more reflective of today's rates than the National Writer's Union's $20,560.

In a letter published in *The New York Times Book Review*, Christopher Lasch, a writer who taught at my alma mater (the University of Rochester) when I was an undergraduate there, observed: "The advances paid to most writers have declined. Publishers prefer to publish blockbusters or would-be blockbusters instead of taking a chance on a book that may take several years to find an audience."

And in *The American Twenties* (Lippincott), a book about America in the 1920s, author John K. Hutchens reports, "In the 1920s, the newcomer had less difficulty getting into print than he has now. The first printing was apt to be small. Probably the publisher expected to lose money, but he was investing in the author's future, a speculative gesture he cannot so often afford today."

Ironically, publishers' ability to determine which books will be best-sellers is limited. On the July 15, 1996 *New York Times Book Review* best-seller list, for example, were, predictably, such books as a bio of John and Jacqueline Kennedy, a bio of Bill and Hillary Clinton, two books about the O.J. Simpson trial, Dennis Rodman's memoirs, and a book on Whitewater. But some of the books on the list were surprises — most notably, *The Cloister Walk* by Kathleen Norris, described as "a poet's experiences at a monastery" ... hardly typical best-seller material. Another surprise was *Undaunted Courage* by Stephen E. Ambrose, a history book about the Lewis and Clark expedition.

Your advance will probably be in the low to medium-end of the range quoted by National Writers Union. The exception would be if your publisher thinks your book will be a block-buster best-seller. In that case, the sky's the limit, and your advance might range from $25,000 to $100,000 or more. But that's rare.

Advances for the average nonfiction book of $5,000 or $10,000 or $15,000 are more typical ... and that's what you should expect.

As a rule of thumb (but a very imprecise rule), most publishers offer an advance equal to the anticipated first year's royalties. So if your royalty is $1 per book, and they offer a $5,000 advance, that indicates they expect to sell about 5,000 copies within 12 months of the "pub date" (date the book is officially released).

What if the advance is not high enough? You or your agent can always ask for more. But again, be realistic. If the publisher offers $15,000, you might be able to get the advance up to $17,000 or $18,000 by asking for more. But it would be unlikely that a publisher whose initial offer is $15,000 can be negotiated up to, say, $25,000 or $30,000. Generally with advances in the range discussed ($5,000 to $15,000), the best you can do is get another couple of thousand dollars or so.

It is possible that the publisher will stand firm and not offer a higher advance. What then? If you have other offers, take them. If not, you have to evaluate whether you should go ahead despite the low offer.

To some authors, books have value beyond the advances and royalties they earn. Perhaps publication of the book will gain you tenure or help promote your professional practice. Or getting that first book is so important to you that you're willing to put up with a so-so offer.

That's not necessarily a bad strategy: Having a book published can open lots of doors for you in writing as well as in other areas. People perceive authors as experts, so getting the book published can do a lot to enhance your reputation and bring you fame.

If you are offered a too-low advance, and the publisher won't go higher, then negotiate better terms on the rest of the contract. Especially your royalties. If you believe the book will sell well, go for a higher royalty in lieu of a bigger advance. If you sell your books directly or give them away (e.g., back of the room sales at seminars you speak at, giving books as a premium to clients), ask the publisher to give you a lot of extra free copies. Remember, the retail value of 100 free copies of a $20 book is $2,000.

Is a very low advance (say, under $5,000) a bad sign? In a way, yes. The higher the advance, the greater the publisher's investment in, and commitment to, the book. Yet a big advance is no guarantee of a best-seller. Many books publishers have put a lot of money behind have bombed, while others that got small advances and zero promotion dollars have become mega-hits.

You will get a check for half the advance upon signing of your book contract; the balance will be paid when you hand in the manuscript and the publisher considers it acceptable.

Since "acceptable" is a subjective term, couldn't the publisher just say your book is unacceptable and on that basis refuse to pay the balance of your advance? Yes.

Is this grossly unfair to the author and does it totally favor the publisher? Yes. Can you negotiate this "acceptability" clause out of your book contract? No. So don't even try. Learn to live with it. Wait until you're a superstar best-selling author. Then you may have enough clout to negotiate this clause out. Otherwise, forget it.

➤ *ROYALTIES* **(GROSS vs. NET).** The royalty is the amount of money the author receives per book sold. There are two types of royalties: gross (the more common) and net.

A *gross royalty* means the author's payment is a percentage of the *retail price* of the book. If you have a 10 percent royalty on a $10 book, you would get $1 for every copy sold.

A *net royalty* means the author's payment is a percentage of the *amount of money the publisher is paid* for the book — not the suggested retail price. Since many copies are sold at a discount off their cover price, a net royalty is less favorable to you, the author, than a gross royalty — and therefore you should either try to get a gross royalty or ask for higher percentages if the royalty is on a net basis.

Bookstores, for example, typically buy books from publishers at a discount of 40 to 45 percent off the cover price. If the discount is 40 percent, the publisher would collect $6 for a $10 book. A royalty of 10 percent net would give the author 60 cents (10 percent of $6) vs. $1 for a gross royalty.

As a rule, whenever a publisher offers a net royalty instead of a gross royalty, they are effectively cutting your royalty in half.

➤ *HARDCOVER ROYALTIES:* A typical hardcover royalty is 10 percent for the first 5,000 sold, 12 1/2 percent for the next 5,000 sold, and 15 percent for all copies over 10,000 sold (this is gross, not net).

While most publishers will not negotiate for higher percentages, you can ask for (and sometimes get) the royalty to accelerate a little faster. For example, you could ask for the royalty to jump from 12.5 to 15 percent after 7,500 copies are sold instead of 10,000 copies. Some publishers will say okay to this.

➤ *TRADE PAPERBACK ROYALTIES:* As defined earlier, trade paperbacks are larger "quality" paperbacks sold mainly in bookstores and via mail order. Average price is around $11. Gross royalties on trade paperbacks range from 6 to 10 percent, with 7 or 8 percent being typical.

➤ *MASS MARKET ROYALTIES.* Mass market paperbacks are the smaller paperbacks sold in drug stores and supermarkets and airports as well as bookstores. Average price is around $5. Gross royalties on mass market editions range from 6 to 15 percent. The royalty may escalate depending on number of copies sold.

➤ *MAIL ORDER ROYALTIES.* The above royalty rates apply to bookstore sales. For copies sold via mail order, the royalty is typically 5 percent of gross for both hardcover and paperback books.

➤ *FIRST AND SECOND SERIALIZATION.* "First serialization" refers to the fee you and the publisher are paid by a magazine which reprints a portion of your book as an article prior to the book's publication.

"Second serialization" refers to fees paid to you by magazines which reprint portions of your book as articles after the book is published.

The fees vary widely depending on which magazine or newspaper is buying serial rights. For example, the *Los Angeles Times* recently paid $400 for second serial rights to a portion of my book, *How To Sell, Your House, Co-op, Or Condo. Cosmopolitan* paid $750 to run a condensed chapter of my book *Creative Careers* as an article in their magazine.

Your book contract will indicate what percentage of serialization fees go to you and what percentage go to the publisher. A 50/50 arrangement is standard, but you can always ask for more.

Try asking for 90/10 or, if your advance is small, ask for 100/0 in your favor. Expect to end up getting between 50 and 75 percent of first and second serial.

Note that unless your book is a blockbuster, you are more likely to make second serial sales than first serial; therefore you should concentrate on getting a higher split of payment on second serial, and not worry so much about first serial.

➤ *DRAMATIC AND AUDIOVISUAL RIGHTS* refers to fees paid by studios or producers for the right to turn your book into a movie TV show. This is a possibility for books that are biographies, journalism, or other books that tell a dramatic story.

"Audiovisual rights" refers to fees paid by companies for the right to turn your book into a video or audio cassette program. This is most likely with instructional and how-to books.

"Electronic rights" refers to publishing your book on the World Wide Web, CD ROM, disk, or other electronic medium. There is a lot of controversy and in-fighting between writers and publishers on who owns electronic rights. As a rule of thumb, the more you retain the better. On the other hand, despite all the hype about the Internet, few authors are making much money from Web publishing of books right now. See Chapter 13 for more information on the Internet and electronic book publishing.

Typical contracts split these rights 50/50, but you can frequently ask for and get a higher percentage, especially if the publisher doesn't feel these rights will sell and you do (often, knowing your market better, you are right and they are wrong). For my how-to books, I always try to get 90 to 100 percent of audiovisual rights, since audio cassettes are a natural medium for how-to information (my book, *Selling Your Services*, was made into an audio cassette album by Blackstone Publishing).

➤ ***BOOK CLUB SALES.*** These are fees you get for sales to book clubs. Usually split 50/50. Most publishers won't budge much on this one.

➤ ***TRANSLATIONS AND FOREIGN EDITIONS.*** Most U.S. publishers just distribute to the U.S. and some to Canada. Therefore your book may attract overseas publishers who want to do a foreign-language edition for sale in their country.

Your contract spells out which foreign rights are included in the publisher's purchase of rights to your work, and which you reserve. The more foreign rights you can hold on to, the better. Be warned that royalty payments from foreign publishers are often spotty or even nonexistent. The advance may be the only compensation you ever see, aside from the addition of a foreign language edition of your book to your personal library.

➤ ***MANUSCRIPT PREPARATION AND ACCEPTANCE.*** The contract will say things like the manuscript must be double-spaced, you must hand in the original and one photocopy, and so on. Minor details, easily complied with.

But the contract will also have a clause saying that the publisher is obliged to pay your advance and publish your book only if they find the manuscript "acceptable".

This is a clause that is unfair to authors, as "acceptable" is a vague and subjective judgment. Therefore, this clause gives the publisher a legal "out" if they decide for any reason they don't want to publish your book once you hand it in.

The publisher will insist on this clause and you will not be able to negotiate its deletion. So if you want to be a book author, learn to live with this clause. I have. So can you.

➤ **VISUALS.** Part of the clause on manuscript preparation will say that providing illustrations is the author's responsibility.

This is not a problem with the majority of adult books that are mainly text and have little or no photos or diagrams. If that describes your book, don't worry about visuals.

But if your book is heavily dependent on visuals, discuss this up-front with your publisher. Will the cost of preparing visuals come out of your advance, or will they foot the bill? The contract must be explicit, or you could end up spending your advance and more to pay for drawings and photos for your own book!

The publisher will sometimes prepare at no cost to you diagrams, tables, and other simple visual displays that are mostly lines and text. But any diagram, drawing, sketch, or photo is normally the author's responsibility. And visuals can be expensive.

My solution is not to do books that are heavily dependent on visuals which eliminates the whole problem. And 95 percent of adult books fall into this category.

On children's picture books, the publisher will probably team you with an illustrator, and the two of you will split advance and royalties 50/50.

➤ **DELIVERY.**  Your contract will specify a due date by which you must hand in the completed manuscript.

For an average-length nonfiction book, most publishers will give you 4 to 9 months to write it. On bigger books, you may be able to get more time. But a 4 to 9-month schedule is the most common.

➤ **AUTHOR'S WARRANTY.**  This is a clause which says you are the original author of all the material in your book, and that you didn't plagiarize or steal copyrighted material from other works. (Acceptable use of material from other sources is covered in the next chapter.) If you have taken copyrighted material from other sources, the publisher will require you to obtain a signed permission form from the copyright holder (see appendix C) and provide a copy of the form to the publisher along with your manuscript.

➤ **OPTION.**  An option clause says the publisher has the right of first refusal on your next book.

This means you must show your next book proposal to the publisher first on an exclusive basis. If the publisher is not interested, you can go ahead and market the book elsewhere. If they make an offer, you can show the book to other publishers, but you have to give the current publisher a chance to match and better other offers. If the publisher does make the best offer, you are obligated to let them publish the book.

Most novice writers like the sound of this and think an option is to their benefit. But I don't like option clauses, and ask for them to be deleted from all of my contracts. I suggest you do likewise. The reason is that an option ties you up.

For instance, you may have a hot idea for a second book while working on the first. Without an option clause, you can go ahead, develop that idea, and sell it to another publisher while working on your current book. But with an option clause, you have to go to your current publisher with the idea first. And the option will state that they don't have to consider the new proposal until the current book is finished and accepted.

The end result is that you are forced to delay a potentially lucrative new project for up to 9 months because of the option clause. In that time, you may lose interest, or another author may beat you to the market with a similar book. For this reason, I consider options a negative, and this is one point on which I am fairly inflexible.

If the publisher insists on an option clause, make it specific rather than general. If you are writing a science book, change the contract clause to read that the publisher has an option only on the next science book you write. This means you can write and sell a humor book to another publisher while working on your science book without violating the option clause.

➤ **COPYRIGHT.** The contract will probably have a clause stating that the publisher will copyright the book in your name. If the clause should say that the publisher will copyright the book in its own name, have it changed so that you become the copyright holder. This is important if the book goes out of print and you want to publish it yourself or sell it to another publisher.

➤ **TERMINATION.** The termination clause states that if the book goes out of print, all rights revert to the author.

This is an essential clause, so make sure it's there. If you sign a contract without a termination clause, the book could go out of print, and you would legally be unable to get it back into print with your own edition or through another publisher. The work you created would be in limbo forever (or at least until the copyright runs out, at which time anyone who pleases can print and publish copies of the book).

➤ **REMAINDERS.** The remainder clause, often combined with the termination clause, states that if the book goes out of print, the author is to be notified and given the opportunity to buy any unsold copies in the publisher's inventory, or "remainders," at a low price. Sometimes the price is specified (e.g., "cost plus 10 percent" would mean a book that retailed for $15 but cost $3 per copy to manufacture would be sold for $3.30 apiece to the author); sometimes it is not.

Be sure the contract discusses remainders and that you have first right to buy remaining inventory; many authors benefit by getting lots of copies of their book at low cost. You can use them as giveaways or sell them at cover price plus shipping and handling via mail order.

➤ **AUTHOR'S COPIES AND DISCOUNT.** "Author's copies" refers to the number of free copies of the book the publisher gives the author upon publication. Ten is standard, but this is one of the most negotiable points, and I have gotten as many as 100 or more.

"Author's discount" refers to the discount at which you can buy additional copies of your book from the publisher. Forty percent is standard, but you can easily negotiate this to 50 percent or slightly higher.

➤ **ADDITIONAL TERMS AND CLAUSES.** Appendix E contains the actual publisher's contract for my book, *Selling Your Services*. Skim it to get a better appreciation for the fine points and small print of book contracts. We've annotated it to highlight some of the more important contract points.

# CHAPTER 10

# WRITING AND DELIVERING THE MANUSCRIPT

Okay. You've negotiated the terms, agreed to a deadline date for delivery of the manuscript, have signed the book contract, and the publisher has returned a signed copy to you or your literary agent with a check for half your advance. Now what?

Now the work of writing a book, editing, rewriting, and getting it published begins.

"Being a writer of nonfiction books doesn't seem perishingly difficult," says John Jerome in his book, *The Writing Trade* (New York: Lyons & Burford, 1992). "It just requires a certain amount of energy and an intelligent interest in the world ... and a certain accumulated skill at organizing the materials that one's research gathers."

On the other hand, writing is what stops many potential authors from getting their book ideas into print. As poet May Sarton observes, there are many people who want to have written a book, but far fewer who want to do the actual writing.

"If you intend to be a writer, you must write," says author Jo Frohbieter-Mueller in an article in *New Writer's Magazine* (December 1995, p. 10). "We all know people who talk about writing but they never get around to actually writing. To become a published author, you must write."

Adds the late Erma Bombeck (Daily News, January 31, 1996): "It is probably true that every person has a book in him fighting to get out. The wanna-be writer has to commit. Stop talking about clever titles and get the book written."

Since you already know how to write, I won't go into great detail. But I will hit the highlights of this process.

## GETTING YOUR EDITOR'S COMMENTS ON
### YOUR PROPOSAL AND OUTLINE

"The editor's task is the humble one of shepherding the author through the often long and frequently lonely process of writing a book and subsequently sending the book out to make its way in the world," says book editor Gregory Payne (*Bioscience*, March 1995). The first step in this process is to discuss your content outline and proposal with your editor.

Does she want you to write the book exactly as you described it? Often the editor will suggest or ask for changes. She may suggest a different title or subtitle. She may want you to include certain specific information. She might ask you to add one or more chapters, expand certain topics, delete others.

Some of these will be suggestions or recommendations, others more along the lines of a request or demand. How negotiable are these?

You'll find that most editors are pretty flexible. They recognize that you, as the author, know your topic better than they do. At the same time, they are more experienced in producing books, and have a good feel for what would make your book better, even though they are not experts in the subject. So listen ... and benefit from their years of experience in the publishing industry.

What if you do not want to make a suggested change? First, consider the source of your resistance. Is the suggestion truly bad ... or are you resistant because it's extra work and you don't feel like doing it? The former is a good reason to argue; the latter is a poor one.

Keep in mind that the "acceptable manuscript" language in your contract gives the publisher power to reject your book and not pay you the advance if they deem your manuscript unsatisfactory. Therefore it is in your best interest to work with your editor to deliver a book that pleases you both.

## HOW TO SET UP A FILE FOLDER SYSTEM FOR COLLECTING RESEARCH MATERIALS FOR EACH CHAPTER

Many authors, including me, use the file-folder system for current and future book projects. Here's author Mortimer Adler to explain it:

"I prepare a file folder for each chapter, and I place materials into those files as I think of them or come across data for them." (Source: *Information Marketing Report*, February 2, 1993, page 10).

Make your chapter folders, using ordinary manila file folders, as soon as you've written your content outline (see chapter 5 for instructions on writing a content outline). Print or photocopy an extra copy of the full content outline. Then, with scissors and tape, cut it up and paste the description of each chapter (the title and bullet points) on the outside front of the file folder for that chapter. Put all the chapter folders in a hanging file folder for the book, and place it in a file cabinet drawer.

Now, as you come across news items, human interest stories, statistics, articles, and other data and information that relate to your topic, tear them out, jot them down, or photocopy them and place them in the appropriate file folder.

Do this over the period (usually several months) when you are developing your proposal and then marketing your book to publishers.

When you finally get a go-ahead and sit down to write the book, you will have a wealth of information — probably 80 to 90 percent of all you need at your fingertips. This leisurely, fun method of gathering material eliminates the need to do intensive research in a hurry later, when the book deadline is looming.

## RESEARCH: HOW TO GATHER GOOD MATERIAL

Read widely. Become an information-collector. When you read anything – newspapers, magazines, newsletters, reports – read with scissors and pen at hand. Be on the lookout for statistics, facts, and stories that can enhance your manuscript.

When you see something of interest, clip it. Note the source publication, page, date, year, title, and author in pen on the clipping. Then drop it in the appropriate chapter file.

You can file it without reading it; read it later. If you do read it now, use a yellow highlighter to highlight appropriate material. This saves you the trouble of reading the entire piece a second time when you're working on that chapter. With the actual articles in your files, rather than just notes, "dates, quotations, and myriad other details can be rechecked as often as need be, thus minimizing the number of inadvertent errors that steal into a manuscript," says biographer and historian Gale E. Christian (*The Writer*, May, 1995).

A similar research method is used for radio and television. Jot down any interesting information you hear on radio, noting the date, time, and station. If a TV show is going to cover or discuss your topic, put a blank tape in the VCR and record it. If the show offers transcripts for sale, order the transcript and put it in your chapter file.

Keep pad and pen handy wherever you go. When you overhear dialogue, see an event, or come up with an idea that relates to the book, jot it down. When you get home, into the appropriate chapter file it goes.

### Fair Use of Material from Other Books and Articles

What about using material from other published works? Do you need to obtain permission? How do you do so? Must you cite the source if you paraphrase rather than quote or copy word for word?

Use of copyrighted materials is a subject best left to the attorneys, and you may want to consult yours. I cannot begin to adequately cover the subject here; you could write an entire book on copyright, and several people have.

So let me briefly touch on the key points only. Please keep

in mind that I am not an attorney and cannot give you legal advice. What follows is for general information only; and before you take action, the advice of a competent professional should be sought.

### KEY POINTS CONCERNING USE OF COPYRIGHTED MATERIAL

You can copyright sentences but not ideas. Therefore it is permissible to express an idea presented in another source in your own words.

When expressing the ideas of another author in your own words, you should as a courtesy credit the source with a reference or footnote if the ideas are unique or original with that author. If the idea is common knowledge and has been expressed by many others, no reference is required.

Copyright law permits "fair use" of another's material in your own; even experts are unclear as to what constitutes fair use. One major publisher told me you are allowed to use up to 50 words from an article and up to 300 words from a book without the copyright owner's consent or permission. Of course you should credit the source.

If you use more than 50 words from an article or more than 300 from a book, get the copyright owner's permission in writing. This is done by sending a "permissions form" to the magazine publisher or book publisher, to the attention of the Permissions Editor (you can address it by title; no need to find out the editor's name). Appendix C contains a sample permission form you can adapt to suit your needs.

You cannot use any text from a poem or song, even two or three words, without obtaining permission using a permission form. The same goes for cartoons, drawings, photographs, illustrations, and tables. If you took the photo yourself, and a person is in it, you must get that person's signed permission to use his or her likeness in your book.

Some sources will give you permission to use their material at no cost as long as you credit them as the source. Others may charge a fee, usually but not always small (from $25 to $125 or so).

## WRITE THE BOOK IN SECTIONS

Create a writing schedule and stick with it. Break the project of writing the book into small bite-size tasks. This makes it easier and keeps you on schedule.

You've already made your content outline, as shown in chapter 5. And your chapter files should be crammed with source material by now, if you've done what I've suggested. Now all that remains is the writing. The planning, organization, and research has already been done with the content outline and chapter files.

Go to your computer file containing the book proposal and content outline. Now duplicate it, making each chapter in the content outline a separate computer file.

Open the file for the first chapter you intend to write. The chapter title in your content outline file becomes the main heading for the chapter (e.g., "Chapter 1: Setting Up Your Fish Tank"). The bullets (•) from the content outline become subheads; just take out the bullets or asterisks and underline or boldface each subhead.

Now you are ready to write. You fill in text under each subhead, and before you know it, you've written a book.

How will your writing schedule look? How much will you have to write each day?

The average nonfiction book is 200 book pages, which is equivalent to 320 pages of double-spaced typed manuscript. If you have 15 chapters, each chapter will be 21 pages typed double-spaced. If each chapter has, say, 5 to 9 major sections, each with its own subhead, each section you must write will be approximately three or four manuscript pages, or about 1,000 words maximum.

You have 9 months to complete the book. If you do two chapters a month, you finish in 7 1/2 months - a month and a half ahead of schedule. (You can use the extra time to edit and polish the manuscript until it's just right.)

At two chapters a month, you must write 42 pages of manuscript a month, or about 10 pages a week. That comes out to two typed pages a day — about 500 words per day. That is not a big challenge, and you can easily do it even if you hold a full-time job during the day. Remember, you will have time at the end to edit and polish, so the two pages don't have to be perfect.

This schedule assumes you work five days a week on the book and take two days off. Writers who hold day jobs might not write during the week but might do five pages on Saturday and five on Sunday.

Ted Nicholas, author of the best-selling book *How to Form Your Own Corporation Without a Lawyer for Under $75*, has his own suggested schedule. He recommends you write three double-spaced typewritten pages a day, 6 days a week. The pages do not have to be perfect, because you can edit and rewrite later.

"The important thing is to get the ideas down on paper," says Nicholas in the *Direct Marketing Success Letter, Special Edition*. "Make sure you complete three pages no matter what." Following this plan, you will have a finished book in 3 to 4 months.

Three pages is approximately 750 words. Can you write 750 words a day? Yes, you can. Charles Harold St. John Hamilton, listed in the *Guinness Book of World Records* as the most prolific author of all time, wrote 80,000 words a week, or more than 10,000 words (40 pages of double-spaced typed manuscript) a day — a total of 75 million words during his career, all without a PC or word processor.

If you don't like setting page or word goals, Nicholas recommends you write for 2 hours a day, 6 days a week. "Sometimes people are more productive using specific time as a daily goal. For many writers, blocks of time set aside is a better inducement for them in completing a book than anything else."

### WHAT TO DO IF YOU WANT TO STRAY FROM YOUR BOOK PROPOSAL'S ORIGINAL OUTLINE

As you work on the book, you may find that the content outline in your original proposal, which you wrote with an eye toward persuading a publisher to buy your book, is not perfect.

You may want to add material, change section and chapter headings, reorganize sections and chapters, or omit material you originally said you would include.

Generally the editor won't care if you don't stick exactly to your original outline; they know the initial outline was just that — an initial outline — and their authors routinely make modifications as they go along.

So if you want to do things that stray from your original proposal, just go ahead and do them. No need to conference with the editor and discuss every little change.

The exception would be a major change that makes the book substantially different than what the editor believed she was buying. In that case, telephone your editor, discuss it, and get their OK before proceeding.

## FINDING THE RIGHT TONE AND STYLE

Don't try to be too literary. Avoid imitating the style of particularly stylish prose writers you admire. For example, many writers who have read ... Tom (*The Right Stuff*) Wolf - suddenly - begin to think that ... hey! ... I want to write just like him! But when you imitate for the sake of imitating, the style becomes too apparent and is distracting to the reader.

The best style is to write naturally and simply. Write clearly and in plain language. Focus on content, not style. Schopenhauer said: "My first rule for a good style is to have something to say; in fact, this in itself is almost enough." (As quoted in *The Art Of Readable Writing* by Rudolph Flesch.)

"I never use a long word when a short one will do or an involved construction when a simple one will do or literary trickery when plain-speaking will do," explains Isaac Asimov, author of more than 475 books. "Doing that, I am capable of convincingly treating my readers as my intellectual equals, and in return for that, they will go to all lengths to understand me."

Best-selling author Sol Stein, in his book *Stein on Writing* (New York: St. Martin's Press, 1995), advises authors to edit and prune their own manuscripts before sending them to the publisher: "As you work along as an editor, do you see any places where you might have padded the manuscript with unnecessary digressions, overly extensive patches of description, or anything else that strikes you as filler? You always strengthen text when you remove the padding."

Adds writing consultant Joe Vitale in *Zen and the Art of Writing:* "Write simply, and your style will rise and flow from within you."

### PREPARING THE FINAL MANUSCRIPT

Once the book is done, go through it several times, rewriting and editing and polishing and proofreading. Hand in as clean a finished manuscript as you can. The cleaner and more polished the finished manuscript, and the less work the editor has to do with it, the happier she'll be.

Manuscripts are typed double-spaced on one side of a sheet of plain white paper. Each new chapter should begin on a separate page. Include a table of contents and title page. Number all pages in sequence in the upper right-hand corner of the page. Have at least one other person proofread the manuscript to catch as many mistakes as possible before you submit it.

Jack Tracy, a nonfiction publisher, gives the following additional suggestions for manuscript format and preparation (originally published in *The Writer*, July 1996):

➤ Use normal type in 10, 11, or 12-point size.

➤ Do not add space between paragraphs.

➤ Indent paragraphs one-half inch.

➤ Do not justify the text.

➤ Use regular paper. Avoid erasable bond.

➤ Put your name, address, and telephone number (or the name, address, and phone of your agent) on the title page.

➤ Do not bind the manuscript. Leave the pages loose.

Make two copies of the manuscript. Send the original and

one copy in a manuscript box, padded envelope, or other cardboard box. Says Tracy, "Do not wrap your submissions so thoroughly that the packaging has to be ripped apart." Keep one copy on file at home.

Although PCs have proliferated, many mainstream NYC publishers do not ask for text on floppy disks and prefer instead to work from a print-out hard copy.

The reason is that the editor wants to keep track of their comments and editorial suggestions, as well as the changes you have made. With post-it notes and changes made directly on the original manuscript without retyping, the editor can see what was done and what wasn't.

When corrections are made on disk, the old version is "gone" and the editor can't tell when and where changes were made. A feature such as the Word for Windows Revision Tool does, in fact, allow you to edit a computer file while showing both the old and new text. Unfortunately, most editors today prefer to edit with a pencil than use a PC.

Almost all book publishers and their editors still work with typed manuscripts, and you are not required to provide diskettes. Some smaller presses may encourage (but not require) electronic submissions; so having a PC is a plus but not mandatory.

Ask the publisher if they want the manuscript as a computer file, and if so, when you should submit this file and what format they prefer. Of those publishers who accept disks, some will want you to submit a disk with the initial manuscript. Others will copy edit the manuscript, then send it back to you, and ask for a disk once you've made the changes.

As noted, many publishers are not yet in the computer age and don't routinely ask for disks. A small but growing minority want disks, but don't insist on it. I am unaware of any major publishing house that insists on a disk, but I wouldn't be surprised if they soon do or if some do already. As more publishers get on the Internet, authors a few years from now will be sending in their completed book manuscripts via e-mail. I've done this already with at least one book, and it's wonderfully convenient and easy.

## MEETING YOUR DEADLINES

Do not miss your deadline. If you do, the publisher can legally get out of the contract, and may want to if you screw up their schedule. If this happens, all your hard work is wasted. Make a writing schedule, stick with it, and meet your deadline.

If it looks like missing the deadline is unavoidable, ask (or have your agent ask) for an extension. Do this as early as possible; not two days before the book is due. Most publishers will grant one or two extensions for anywhere from a month to three or four months. Having an author ask for more time happens fairly frequently, and most publishers tolerate it.

If they grant an extension, send a confirmation letter and keep a copy in your files. Editors change jobs frequently, so you want any changes to the original contract to be in writing.


## HOW TO INCREASE YOUR WRITING PRODUCTIVITY

Marcia Yudkin, prolific author of *Marketing Online* and many other books, offers these tips for increasing your book-writing productivity:

*1. BEGIN WITH THE BIG PICTURE.* It's easier to write when you know roughly which elements need to go where. Begin with an outline. Change and edit as necessary as you go along.

*2. START BEFORE YOU FEEL READY.* If you wait until you know everything there is to know about your topic, you will never get started. Use my file folder method of doing "pre-research," and when you get the publisher's go-ahead, use this information to start writing chapters.

> Keep in mind best-selling author Dr. Spock's advice: *"Trust yourself. You know more than you think you do."*

*3. START ANYWHERE.* Start with any section of any chapter that interests you. Skip around, writing the sections that most interest you, are easiest, or for which you have the most re-search material. Says Yudkin: "Almost any kind of project can be broken down so there's something you can do on it immediately." Break the book into chapters and sections, and do the easy parts first.

I start with the back matter and front matter, writing the routine stuff like acknowledgments, table of contents, and author's bio first. This gives me a feeling of accomplishment and gets some pages down, so the rest seems less daunting.

I also like to set up individual computer files for the front matter, back matter, appendices, and chapters before I start the actual writing. When I'm ready to write, I turn on the PC, open the file for the chapter or appendix I am ready to work on, and just start filling in text. When I am out of material, I flip to another section of the file or to another file. So I am always able to make progress.

*4. LEAVE HOLES TO PLUG UP LATER.* Over-researching can put you off your schedule, so keep writing section and chapters even though you don't have 100 percent of the information. Then determine exactly what and how much information is missing. Go back later and fill in the holes. Don't over-research; just get enough information to plug those holes and fill the information gap. Beware of information overload. Neither you nor your readers need to know every last detail about a particular point. As the writer, it's your job to determine what's most important for the reader to know, and to present it in a clear and interesting fashion.

*5. PICK PEOPLE'S BRAINS.* According to Yudkin it's faster to hitchhike on someone else's expertise than to become an expert yourself. You can read enough to know which questions to ask and which experts to talk to for help. Many experts are easily accessible and will be happy to go over the material for you, fill in the missing pieces, and correct mistakes and misconceptions.

*6. INCUBATE.* Read over written drafts, put them away, and think about your material for a while. New thoughts and ideas will come into your mind. Open your computer files and add them to the sections and chapters where they fit best.

*7. TAKE FREQUENT BREAKS FROM THE BOOK.* If I had nothing to do but this book all day, it would drive me crazy. My preference is to have a number of writing projects in the works simultaneously. When I get burnt out on the book, I can turn to an article and start fresh on a new project. When I've gone as far as I can with the article, I'll go to another project on my list and start that. The variety prevents writer's block, eliminates boredom, and keeps you fresh and enthusiastic.

### ADDITIONAL TIPS FOR WRITING YOUR BOOK

Over the past 16 years I have written more than four dozen books. Here's my best advice on how to do it efficiently, effectively, and enjoyably:

➤ Don't worry about other books on the subject and how your book compares with them as you write your book. Just do the best you can on every page.

➤ Don't feel obliged to tell the reader every fact that exists about your topic. No book can or should do that. Just tell them the best of what you've discovered about the topic — information that is most interesting, most unusual, or most useful.

➤ Don't worry that you didn't "cover it all" when you hand in your manuscript. You can always write another book covering the same topic from a different or more advanced point of view. You can always update your book with a revised second edition.

➤ Don't agonize over every word, but do read, revise, and rewrite your copy until it's as smooth and clear as you can make it.

➤ In writing, there is no one "right answer" as to how to craft a sentence, paragraph, or essay. There are many different ways to do it, and each is right. Therefore, don't agonize over writing a piece of copy this way or that way.

If it seems to be working for you, leave it be.

➤ Don't make your book a carbon copy of the ten other books on your topic already on the market. Your life experience, point of view, interpretations, and unique perspective are what add interest to the book.

➤ While you will not be the focus of most of the books you write, do let your personality shine through in your writing, where appropriate. Nonfiction books are more enjoyable when readers feel the author is speaking to them directly.

➤ Cater to your audience. Most nonfiction books are aimed at specific audiences. If you are writing for computer enthusiasts and you are one, establish that sense of camaraderie in your writing. If you are a computer expert writing for a lay audience, acknowledge and work to overcome their fear and dislike of technology. Stress the benefits they will get and how painless and fun you are going to make mastering the PC for them. Speak directly to your audience and, where possible, establish empathy.

➤ Do not feel under pressure to reveal a great truth or come up with new data in your book. A wise person once said, "Experts don't necessarily know more than other people; they just have their information better organized." Readers read for reinforcement more than anything else. If your information is well organized and clearly expressed, readers will be grateful for it. If you give them one or two new ideas or concepts, they'll consider it a bonus.

➤ Aim for clarity and conciseness. Choose words carefully. Edit sentences to ensure a smooth flow from thought to thought. But don't agonize over your copy to an unnatural degree in a misguided effort to create a literary masterpiece. Keep in mind this advice from writer Lou Redmond: "Nobody writes as well as he or she would like to. We just write as well as we can." Write as well as you can, and the result will be a book of which you will be pleased and proud to be the author.

# CHAPTER 11

# FOLLOWING UP

Handing in your manuscript is a great relief to most authors; they feel that the difficult part is over, and now the fun begins.

While it's true you're through the toughest parts of the publishing process — selling and writing the book — there's still some work to be done. Let's take a look at what happens from the time you hand in your manuscript until the month your book is published.

## 'PUB DATES'

Your editor will assign a publication date ("pub date") to your book. This is the formal "coming out" date for your book and is generally set for three to four months later than the actual date your books will be printed and shipped. This advance dating is done to enable the publisher to begin his publicity campaign including sending books out to book reviewers prior to the official publication date.

It generally takes a mainstream publisher 4 to 9 months to produce and print books from the date they are handed in. If you hand in your typed manuscript in January or February, for example, the publisher will probably schedule publication for the autumn of that same year. If you hand in your book in November of this year, the pub date will probably be scheduled for spring of the following year.

## EDITS AND REVISIONS

Rarely will your book be printed exactly as you've written

it. Most likely, there will be changes suggested by several people, including your editor, the copyeditor, and perhaps a third-party ("peer reviewer").

These changes may be minor, or they may be extensive.

When the manuscript is received by the publishing company, your editor will read it and make comments directly on the manuscript, usually using stick-on notes.

The manuscript will be given back to you with the request that you make these changes directly on the manuscript. Some changes will be easy; others may require more research or additional writing.

Make all the changes you can make and feel comfortable with. If you disagree with some of the suggestions, call the editor and discuss it. The editor may come to see your point and agree that the change is not needed.

Sometimes you and the editor will not see eye-to-eye on a point. Unless the comment requires an extraordinary amount of what you consider unnecessary work or is very harmful to the integrity of the book, go ahead and make these changes, even if you don't agree with them.

Editors like authors who are easy to work with; word of an author who is difficult or a prima donna quickly spreads and can hurt your chances for future sales.

My experience is that authors (including me) can be lazy and a bit arrogant and tend to resist comments and criticism from editors. However, I find that most of the criticisms my editors make are valid; most of their suggestions are helpful; and most of their changes result in a better book than I originally handed in.

My advice is therefore to have an open mind and work with editors in the spirit of cooperation rather than see them in an adversarial role. You are allies with a mutual goal: the best book possible.

## COPY EDITING

Once the editor makes her editorial changes, and you do rewrites based on her comments, the book will be sent to a copy editor.

While the editor edits primarily for content, organization, and readability, the copy editor makes sure spelling, punctuation, and grammar are correct and conform to the style of that particular publishing house (e.g., writing "freelance" instead of "free-lance").

You will be given a chance to review the copy editor's work to see if you agree with it. As a rule, I don't agonize over copy editing unless the copy editor made a change that alters my meaning; then I change it back or discuss it with the editor.

## PEER REVIEW

A few mainstream publishers send nonfiction manuscripts to one or more experts in the topic of the book for review and comment; most do not. Textbook, scholarly, and academic publishers, on the other hand, almost always do peer reviews.

Peer reviews are sometimes useful and sometimes not. They are useful when the reviewer has no vested interest and is making suggestions in the spirit of improving the book.

Peer reviews are not useful when the reviewer uses them as an opportunity to show he is the expert and that you are wrong, and too not-so-subtly suggest to your publisher that he could write a much better book.

Editors are generally good at recognizing biased vs. unbiased peer reviews. If you feel a peer review is biased, unfair, and geared toward tearing down the author rather than helping the book, let your editor know, and she will probably give you latitude to ignore any comments not deemed helpful.

## PROOFING OF GALLEYS

After editor review, peer review, rewrites, and copy editing, your manuscript will go into production for typesetting.

Ask the editor if you can review a few samples pages before the entire book is typeset. This way, if you don't like the type (e.g., it's hard to read or too small), you can discuss it with the editor and perhaps get a different typeface and page design.

Once the book is typeset, you will get galleys (copies of the typeset manuscript) to read and check for typos and other errors.

At this stage you should be making corrections only if you find errors or feel the change is absolutely essential, because once the book is in galleys, changes cost money. In fact, most book contracts indicate that any changes to the galleys the author makes other than minor corrections come out of the author's royalties. However, if I feel I have to make a change, I do it. I want the book to be right, and feel it's worth the penalty payment.

## PAGE PROOFS

The galleys will be corrected, cut into pages, and bound with a plain cover as "page proofs." Some of these will be sent by the publisher to authorities in your field for comments (blurbs) the publisher can use on the cover of the finished book.

One copy of the page proofs will be sent to you. This is your last chance to proofread again and catch any remaining errors. You should also check the page proofs carefully to make sure all pages are in correct order and that none are misplaced or left out.

## INDEX

Another copy of the page proofs will be sent to a professional indexer who will create the index for your book. The fee is usually $300 to $500 and is charged against the author's royalty; in other words, the publisher doesn't even pay for the index to your book; you do!

If you want to avoid this charge, tell the publisher you will prepare your own index, and do so. I personally do not like to prepare the index and feel I wouldn't do as good a job as a professional. It's boring work, and time consuming, too. I'd rather let a pro handle it and pay the fee. You may feel differently, of course.

## COMPLETING YOUR AUTHOR'S QUESTIONNAIRE

The publisher's publicity department will send you an author's questionnaire to fill out. Appendix G shows a sample questionnaire.

Most authors find this an annoying chore and do it quickly and without much thought.

Don't make this mistake. The publicity people — the ones responsible for marketing your book through reviews, interviews, and other media exposure — won't have time to read your book. Or even your proposal.

The author's questionnaire – and your answers – is their only source of information about your book. So it's essential that you fill it out as completely and thoroughly as possible. Even if it involves some work on your part.

One technique that makes it faster and easier to complete the author's questionnaire is not to fill in the physical form they send you, but to open a computer file and recreate the form on your disk, typing in all the questions, and then your answers. If you have a scanner, scan the questionnaire into a PC file, then type in your answers.

Many of the answers to questions the PR department asks

have already been written by you and are in the book proposal. You can save a lot of time and labor in filling out the author's questionnaire by importing appropriate text blocks from the proposal into your author's questionnaire

## WORKING WITH THE PUBLICITY DEPARTMENT

The publicity department of the publishing house will send out a press release and perhaps arrange a few radio interviews for you. Big multi-city author's tours are rarer and rarer, and are done mostly for bestselling authors with blockbuster books.

"Well-tailored PR can make many middle-level books profitable," writes Richard Turner in *New York* magazine (June 17, 1996). "You have to work a book, or it won't get discovered."

Be as cooperative as you can when the publicity department asks you to do a radio interview, speak at a convention, do a bookstore autograph party, or whatever. These folks have too many books and authors to deal with, and if you are picky, difficult, or abrupt with them, they will stop putting forth effort on your behalf, and publicity for your book will dry up.

If the publicity department is open to ideas and seems to want you to participate more pro-actively in planning the promotion of your book, do so. On the other hand, if they prefer to keep you at arm's length, you'll probably have to live with that. If you push them, they'll consider you a "difficult" author and give your book minimal attention.

## HOW INVOLVED SHOULD YOU GET IN BOOK PROMOTION?

Most authors I talk with feel their publishers don't do enough to market and promote their book, and with 50,000 new books published each year, this may be true. One reason why authors turn to self publishing (see chapter 12) is the ability to control book promotion and put as much time, effort and money into it as they deem appropriate.

Since my books have all been with traditional publishers, my approach to book promotion is as follows:

1. Do everything the publisher asks you to do to promote your book — from signing autographs in a bookstore to doing early morning call-in radio shows. As I was working on this chapter, I took 10 minutes out to do a short radio interview over the phone with WOSH, a West Coast radio station, in which I discussed Star Trek (promoting my new Star Trek trivia book, *Why You Should Never Beam Down in a Red Shirt*).

Frankly, I'm skeptical that many of the things I do to publicize my books, such as radio interviews, result in a lot of book sales. But I don't bring this up with the publisher. I do everything I am asked willingly and pleasantly. After all, if I am not enthusiastic about promoting my book, why should I expect the publisher to be?

2. If you have good ideas for promotion, suggest them to the publicist or your editor. Follow up to see what's been done. But don't insist. Remember, they, not you, took on the financial risk of publishing the book. It is their property, and since they put the money into it, they have the right to decide when, where, and how much to promote it.

Of course you want your book promoted, but do not overestimate the value of promotion. Sometimes a good but underpromoted book finds an audience and sells truckloads of copies. And even great promotion usually will not sell a book the public is not interested in buying.

3. If you feel one of your promotional ideas is great, and the publisher won't do it, and it won't cost a fortune, consider doing it yourself. If it works, it may bring you some fleeting fame and additional book sales. If not, it's a good learning experience.

However, for a traditionally published book, be careful of spending too much of your own money on promotion. Remember, if a reader buys your book for $10 at a bookstore, you get $1 or less; the publisher, wholesaler and retailer get the other $9. Since you are only getting a small fraction of the money, you cannot be expected to spend a lot of money promoting your book.

If your book is on a hot or timely topic, or has best-seller potential, and the publisher is not treating it accordingly, you may decide to make an exception and promote it more heavily on your own. Establish a budget, and stick with it. Some of the book doctors in Appendix K can advise you on book marketing and promotion.

## A FEW MISCELLANEOUS OBSERVATIONS
### ON BOOK PROMOTION

➤ Do not do promotion until the book is in the book stores. If you do a promotion and the book is not yet in the stores, it's a waste — almost no sales will be made. When the reader sees you on TV or hears you on the radio, they want to be able to go to the bookstore and buy the book that day. If it's not available, they will not tell the bookstore to order the book and call them when it comes in. They will just forget about it and get something else.

➤ If your book is not widely available in bookstores, and you plan to do radio and TV publicity, you must have a toll-free phone number for taking book orders. Make sure the radio talk show host mentions or allows you to mention the toll free phone number several times. Make sure the TV show mentions and shows the phone number several times.

Once, a friend of ours went on Oprah Winfrey to promote her self published book. It is not available in bookstores, and Oprah did not give the toll free order number. The appearance resulted in only a handful of books sold. Yet according to a recent article in *Publisher's Weekly*, many authors whose books are more readily available sell thousands of copies after appearing on this show.

➤ While the advice of talking up your book on the Internet seems sensible, and is something I would do, the fact is the Internet is yet unproven as a medium for selling books in large quantities. Don't set your on-line sales expectations unreasonably high.

➤ Get tapes of your radio and TV appearances. Keep a list of all radio and TV stations and shows on which you are featured. This list, as it grows, will make other radio and TV stations more likely to book you. Keep this list as a permanent reference file on your computer.

➤ Get clippings of all reviews and articles written about your book — originals rather than photocopies, if possible. Make a montage or paste-up of these articles on a sheet of paper. You can use this in future book promotions and to sell your next book to your publisher or another publisher.

➤ Give complete answers. When a reporter or interviewer asks you a question, answer it fully, so your answer stands alone and can be reprinted or broadcast. Don't just say, "It's in my book" or "You can read it in my book." This is a sure way to ensure that your interview isn't aired or printed, and that you are not invited back.

➤ Keep a file of every media contact who writes about you or has you as a guest on their show. When you have a new book to promote, give this contact list to your publisher and make sure they send a press release or other announcement to the people on your list.

➤ Don't be obsessed with getting in the *New York Times*

*Book Review* in particular or book reviews in general. Feature articles on the subject of your book that prominently mention you and your book are often more valuable than straight reviews.

➤ You'd be surprised at which media generate the most sales. Often it's not what you think. For example, one week the *Kiplinger Letter*, a financial newsletter, ran a short two-sentence blurb praising my book, *The Elements of Business Writing*. The publisher sold 1,000 copies that week, based on that blurb. On the other hand, a feature article on the same book in my local daily newspaper generated no discernible sales results or phone calls to me or the publisher.

➤ Think of innovative ways to talk about your topic. For my book, *The Ultimate Unauthorized Star Trek Quiz Book*, I led "Star Trek Jeopardy" trivia quizzes at local Barnes & Noble stores. At one session, 30 of the 50 people came wearing Star Trek costumes. I was wearing a suit. I told the audience, "The bookstore told me to get dressed up, but apparently I misunderstood their instructions." This got a big laugh and set a jovial tone for the evening.

➤ Not every publicity opportunity will go smoothly. Don't worry about this. Just do the best you can.

For example, a reporter for *U.S.A. Today* interviewed me about careers based on my career book, *Creative Careers*, published by John Wiley. She primarily wanted employment statistics, which was not the subject of my book and which I could not provide. She became quickly and apparently annoyed, and when her article came out, neither I nor my book were mentioned, and none of my comments were used.

Financial expert Bill Bresnin had me on his radio show to discuss real estate based on a book I had written for Consumer Reports Books, *How to Sell Your House, Co-op, or Condo*. Actually, I had coauthored the book with my wife, and she — not I — was the real estate expert. Unfortunately, Amy dislikes public speaking, so I was doing the interviews alone.

When Bill asked me a question about mortgages he thought I should know the answer to but did not, he became cold and abrupt. I was put on hold during a commercial about ten minutes into my 30-minute segment. A producer came on the phone, said that Bill wanted to thank me for my time, and hung up on me, with 20 minutes left to go. Apparently he felt I was an ignoramus not worthy of appearing on his show. Perhaps he was right.

Despite being an ignoramus, I was able to do fairly well with other radio interviews on *How to Sell Your House, Co-op, or Condo* because most of the information I was asked about was in the book. Since we were on radio, I could quickly flip to the appropriate pages in the book to answer questions, keeping one step ahead of the interviewer and callers. I did especially well on Bernard Meltzer's show, except he kept calling me "Ralph" instead of "Robert."

The most difficult book publicity challenge for me was discussing *How to Sell Your House, Co-op, or Condo* on CNBC. I showed up at the studio with my handy, well-thumbed copy of the book, ready to answer any question. Then I realized: I would be on camera and unable to reference the book as I talked! Fortunately, all of the questions from the interviewers and callers were questions I had heard and answered on radio shows, so I managed to get through it without embarrassment.

➤ Do what seems right to you. If you love promotion and being interviewed, do as much as you can. If you're not comfortable with it, and prefer to stay behind the word processor instead of in front of the camera or microphone, that's okay too.

➤ But do try to stretch. If you have never given a talk before and in the course of publicizing your book are asked to do so, try it. Even if it makes you nervous. If it goes well, it may open up a whole new field of activity for you. If it doesn't go so well, it will still give you the confidence to try again. And before you know it, you'll be at ease with publicity — an experienced book promotion pro. That can't hurt sales. And can only help your book and your career as an author. Try it. You may actually like it.

# CHAPTER 12

# THE SELF-PUBLISHING OPTION

"Self-publishing" means that you are the publisher as well as the author. You pay to have the book typeset, designed, and printed. You are responsible for storing the inventory, shipping, distribution, sales, marketing, and promotion. As publisher/author, you get to keep all of the revenues generated from sales (less expenses) versus the 6 to 15 percent of sales a mainstream publisher would pay you.

If your goal is to hold in your hands a nicely designed printed book with your name on the cover, self-publishing is relatively easy. Anyone can have a manuscript typeset, take it to a book printer, and pay them to print the books.

If you want to sell a lot of copies of your book, self-publishing requires a long-term commitment on your part. You are your own warehouse, shipping department, accounting department, sales force, publicity department, marketing director, distributor, collections agency, and secretary.

To write a book and have it published by a traditional publisher means you can concentrate on being an author. Self-publishing your book requires that you fulfill all the functions of publisher as well as author. In essence, it means you have to form and run a "mini-publishing company." Are you prepared to make this commitment?

## TRADITIONAL PUBLISHING OR SELF-PUBLISHING?

How do you make the choice between self-publishing versus regular publishing? Unless you are dead set in favor of one particular option — traditional publishing or self-publishing — here are some guidelines to follow.

### GO TO A MAINSTREAM PUBLISHING HOUSE WHEN...

➤ You feel that your idea would have wide appeal to a mass audience.

➤ Yours is the type of book that would sell well in bookstores.

➤ You want the prestige and status that come with selling a book to a "real" publisher.

➤ You do not have the time or inclination to be in business as a small publishing house and would prefer instead to concentrate on writing.

➤ You want to establish yourself and your credentials as a professional writer or as an expert in the topic of the book.

➤ You do not have the skills and expertise to self-publish (e.g., book design, marketing, distribution, desktop publishing) and do not have the desire to acquire them.

### SELF-PUBLISH WHEN...

➤ Your idea appeals to a specialized narrow target market ("slice of a slice"), e.g., parachutists, chiropractors, car wash owners, etc.

➤ Yours is the type of book that would sell well through direct response advertising (magazine ads, direct mail, catalogs, etc.)

➤ The idea of self-publishing appeals to you.

➤ You have the time, talent, and inclination to handle all aspects of the publishing business — distribution, promotion, administrative — in addition to researching and writing

➤ Your book is not a "one-shot" idea, but rather, you plan a whole line of books and related information products (seminars, audio cassettes, videos, special reports, etc.) to educate your chosen target market on various aspects of your topic

➤ The "snob appeal" and status of being published in the conventional method is not important to you, and you won't be bothered by comments from those who look down on self-publishing as something people who can't get published resort to out of desperation (many lay people have this view).

➤ You have been turned down by the major publishing houses, yet believe in the book so strongly that you are willing to act as publisher to see the book get into print and into people's hands.

➤ Self-publishing may also give you another shot at getting a big publisher interested in your book. "If you want to be published by a trade publisher but can't get one interested in your manuscript, you might accomplish your goal by publishing your own book and selling it by mail to prove there is a market for it," writes author Barbara Brabec in *National Home Business Report* (Summer 1993, page 1).

➤ You are impatient and want to get the book out right away, rather than wait the 12 to 18 months it normally takes to write a book and get it published when going through a conventional publisher.

Many proponents of self-publishing (and some are valued colleagues and personal friends of mine) are highly critical of mainstream publishing. They like to promote self-publishing by being negative about big publishing houses. You've heard it before, of course: Big publishing houses are book factories; they are more concerned with making products than marketing products; they destroy your work in the editing process; they don't do a proper job of promoting or publicizing your book; most books don't sell and most authors don't make money.

Then they tell you why self-publishing is better: you, the author, are in control of your material; no uncaring editor will ruin your work; you can properly market and promote your book; you keep all the profits; many self-publishers have become rich by promoting their books and selling via mail or bookstores.

This is all true. To a degree.

But what they don't tell you is the flip side, which gives you a more balanced picture: Namely, that many authors who publish through traditional publishing houses are happy and satisfied with their publishers — at least some of the time. The books bring them fame, prestige, visibility, and enhance their careers. Many have become rich (even millionaires) from royalty payments when their books hit the best-seller lists.

By the same token, there are many people who, lured by the get-rich-quick promises of self-publishing, paid thousands of dollars to print 5,000 copies of their book, proudly gave away copies to family and friends, and now — years after publication — have boxes containing 4,980 copies of their book gathering dust in the attic, basement, or garage.

To self-publish is, in one sense, easier than regular publishing, because it *guarantees* that your book will see print (since *you* are paying to have it printed at a print shop!).

But in another sense, self-publishing is more difficult, because to sell the book you need skills and knowledge in many areas in addition to writing. As we've noted, these include: advertising copywriting, direct mail, small business management, inventory control, purchasing, shipping, distribution, sales, marketing, and many others.

The immediate cash flow in publishing is more favorable for traditional publishing than for self publishing. In traditional publishing, you get an advance of thousands of dollars to put in your bank account before you write the book. And there are virtually no out of pocket expenses.

In self publishing, there is no advance, and the up front

costs — book design, typesetting, printing, and advertising can be considerable, adding up to many thousands of dollars in checks you will write to vendors.

However, if you do decide to self-publish your book, you should be aware of the fact that the newest technologies now allow you to do so for a very nominal cost – as little as a couple of hundred dollars in initial setup costs. This new process is called "print-on-demand."

## PRINT-ON-DEMAND

Up until a couple of years ago, if you decided to self-publish your own book it entailed a print run of several thousand copies and a cost of perhaps $5,000 or even more. Today due to major breakthroughs in publishing technologies, it is entirely possible to print-on-demand any quantity you choose (even a single copy).

If this sounds like something you would be interested in, contact a company called Lightning Source (which is a division of the nation's largest book wholesaler, Ingram, Inc.) You can call them through Ingram at 1-800-937-8100 or directly at 1-615-213-5815.

It is important to note that Lightning Source is a printer and not a publisher. They will print any quantity of books you want but you must pay for, stock and market the books yourself.

Before they can print your book, it must be "camera-ready." That means that even if it is just a computer file, you must have that file prepared to be output as a book. In other words, what prints out of that file is exactly what appears in your book. Lightning Source will not typeset the text, insert page numbers, headers, footers, or indexes. If you are not familiar with these aspects of book preparation, you will have to hire someone to do it for you.

But once this is done you can send them the book either as

a computer file or a laser printed hard copy. They will load the file or scan your hard copy into their computer and turn out a book that is virtually indistinguishable from a book produced by a conventional printer.

Using Lightning Source has an additional benefit that is very important. Since they are a division of Ingram and since most bookstores order their books from Ingram, once your book is in their computer they will actually print your book one at a time as orders come in from the book stores. They will then include your 'just-printed' book along with the rest of that store's order.

What this all means is that although you will pay more for each copy you sell, you do not have to pay for, ship or even stock quantities of books yourself. You can focus all your energies doing the single most important job you will have as a self-publisher...promoting your book. You will need keep on hand only enough books to send to book reviewers, radio and TV media and the like.

Going the route of print-on-demand also means that you can easily test the waters to see just how well your book will sell without making a major financial investment. If the book begins to take off you can then lower your per-book cost by having thousands of copies printed at a conventional printer. Or if you like, you can use the rocketing book sales as leverage in selling your book to a mainline publisher.

One important note: If you do decide self-publishing is for you and that you are willing to undertake the task of promoting your book, one excellent way to generate attention and interest in your book is by doing radio and TV interviews. On-air personalities are always looking for interesting people and topics for their listeners. And one of the most effective ways to get the word out about your book to these on-air hosts, is by advertising in a publication called *Radio & TV Interview Report*. Published three times a month by Bradley Communications, this magazine is mailed to some 4,000 on-air contacts. Their ad rates are reasonable (currently under $500 for a half page.) And for that fee they do all the work including writing the ad, and inserting your photo along with a picture of your book cover. To get a sample issue and to find out more information, call them at 1-800-553-8002.

## NEXT STEPS

*How To Get Your Book Published* focuses on selling your book to a traditional publishing house. In this chapter, we've discussed the nature of self publishing, along with some of the pros and cons. But to provide you with more detailed information on how to self publish is beyond the scope of this book.

The good news is that there have been many excellent books published on "how to get rich by self-publishing books and other printed information and selling them by mail." Since most of these books are written by practitioners, they contain practical information and can help you.

However, not all are equal, and there are certain authors who are considered "gurus" in the self-publishing/book marketing/mail order selling field. If you decide to pursue self-publishing, get and read some of these books first! Here are some of the best ones (please write or call publishers for prices and availability):

*How To Self-Publish Your Book* by Melvin Powers. Wilshire Publishing, Los Angeles, CA. Check your local library. Call 1-800-421-4178. Comprehensive, with lots of detailed information and examples of books and book promotions that worked.

*Mail Order Success Secrets* by Bob Kalian. Roblin Press (1-888-229-3733). How to sell books and other information products by mail. Charmingly written, with solid advice. An invaluable resource if you plan to sell your book through mail order.

*The Self-Publishing Manual* by Dan Poynter. Para Publishing, PO Box 4232, Santa Barbara, CA 93140. Phone: 800-PARA-PUB. Dan is considered the "dean" of self-publishing and his book is the "bible" — detailed, specific, and informative.

*1001 Ways To Market And Promote Your Book* by John Kremer. Ad-Lib Publications, 51 West Adams, Fairfield, Iowa 52556, Phone 515-472-6617. This company has other excellent books for book publishers and those authors who self-publish books and other "information products" and sell them via mail-order.

*How To Publish A Book And Sell A Million Copies* by Ted Nicholas. Nicholas Direct, Inc., 1511 Gulf Blvd., #1, Dept. BB, Indian Shores, FL 33785, phone 813-596-4966. A basic primer on how to self-publish a book and sell it by mail order through direct response ads and direct mail. Nicholas is a successful self-publishing entrepreneur and one of the top direct response ad copywriters of all time. His self-published, self-promoted book, *How To Form Your Own Corporation Without A Lawyer For Under $75*, has sold over a million copies.

*Hypnotic Writing* and *Turbocharge Your Writing* by Joe Vitale. Two excellent books recommended for anyone faced with the challenge of writing a book. Contact: Joe Vitale, P.O. Box 300792, Houston, TX 77230, phone (713) 434-2845. Joe is also available to work with authors on book proposals, manuscripts, self-publishing, and selling to a major publisher.

*How To Make A Whole Lot More Than $1,000,000 Writing, Commissioning, And Selling Information Products* by Jeffrey Lant. Cambridge, MA: JLA Publications, phone 617-547-6372. Detailed, information-packed guide to successful self publishing. Recommended.

*The Complete Guide To Self-Publishing* by Tom and Marilyn Ross (Cincinnati, Ohio: Writer's Digest Books, 1989). One of the standard works in the field. The authors know what they're talking about and explain it clearly.

*Jump Start Your Book Sales* by Marilyn & Tom Ross (Communications Creativity, phone: 1-800-331-8355). Virtually every page of this new book is chuck full of helpful ideas and specific information that will help you get your book into catalogs, make premium sales, do radio interviews and a whole lot more. A great book!

One other point: Traditional publishing and self-publishing are not mutually exclusive. "You're likely to benefit by placing some projects with publishing giants, submitting others to small, specialized companies and maybe even handling some through a tiny company of your own," points out Judith Appelbaum in her book *How to Get Happily Published* (New York: HarperCollins, 1992). "Historically, the roster of self-publishers has included many names that now appear under publishing's most prestigious imprints." She cites as examples Edgar Allan Poe, Mark Twain, and James Fenimore Cooper.

Others include Robert Ringer, author of *Looking Out for Number One* and Roger von Oech, author of *A Whack on the Side of the Head*, who sold the book to Warner Books only after he had sold 30,000 copies himself. My friend Paul Karasik self-published his book on sales, *Sweet Persuasion*, and kept it under his own imprint for several years before selling it to Simon & Schuster. Ted Nicholas, the successful self published author mentioned earlier, says, "The ranks of self-publishers are growing every day." Contemporary authors who have successfully self-published include Dr. William Dyer, Doug Casey, Peter McWilliams, and William Donoghue.

Even bestselling author Stephen King, whose books are published by Viking and New American Library and sell millions of copies, has placed some of his novels with small presses (most notably the Dark Tower series). He has also self-published one of his stories (*The Plant*, which he used as a Christmas gift) and even published stories electronically on the Internet. So you can be both a self publisher and have books come out with small and large mainstream publishing houses. And in the next chapter you will learn about the newest option available to you...publishing online.

# CHAPTER 13

# BOOK PUBLISHING ON THE INTERNET

*"You'd have to be an ostrich not to understand that e-publishing is the wave of the future."*
— Jean Naggar, literary agent to Jean Auel (*Clan of the Cave Bear*), as quoted in *Newsweek* (10/99)

One day in mid-March in the year 2000 the publishing world changed forever when more than 500,000 people went online to buy and download a short story and in doing so created the world's first instant electronic best seller.

The 66 page story, *Riding The Bullet,* written by mega best selling author, Stephen King was in King's words in an interview with Time magazine, a "watershed moment." The short story earned King a minimum of $450,000 without a single drop of ink ever touching paper.

With an estimated 110 million Americans using the Internet, there's no question that this rapidly emerging medium is changing our lives in untold ways. For example, currently more than 10 million people make online purchases every month. And these numbers are growing almost exponentially.

And since books are among the most purchased items on the Internet, this means major changes in the way books are published, distributed and sold. But even more important for authors than book selling via the Internet is paperless book "publishing" via the Internet. By the time you read this chapter, what is described in it will no doubt have already changed. But at least you'll have a starting point from which to pursue your own inquiries.


## PROS AND CONS OF INTERNET PUBLISHING

As a medium, the Internet offers a lot of advantages for book publishing:

• It's easy and inexpensive. Just post your manuscript as a downloadable file on the Web and you're in business. No typesetting or printing costs. No book proposals, query letters, or pursuing agents, editors, and publishers.

• It's scalable. Some books have small audiences. That's a problem with traditional print publishing, where the minimum print runs are usually in the thousands of copies. On the Internet, you can sell as few or as many copies as the market demands, with no minimum production cost. No agonizing over how many copies to print. No books to store and ship; no returns from customers.

• It's quick. From the time you hand your book in to a regular publisher to the time it's available in bookstores can take many months. Internet customers can buy your book the minute you finish the document and post it on the Web.

• It's convenient. The customer can get your book online. No need to order a physical book or search for a bookstore that carries it.

• An online book can more easily be updated and revised than a printed book.

• Books that exist online can be kept "in print" longer then traditional books, which – once they've stopped selling in volume – take up valuable warehouse space needed to hold this year's new books.

Of course, there are disadvantages to Internet book publishing as well:

• Printing out a book manuscript and carrying around the print-out is cumbersome. People still like regular books, which are more portable, attractive, and easier to read.

- The cost of Rocket eBooks and other "electronic books" into which book text can be downloaded from the Internet is still too expensive for some consumers' tastes, although they're rapidly dropping. The electronic books are difficult to read than regular books, although the technology is improving.

- The technology is new, the practice of reading e-books not widely accepted, and only the early innovators are buying and reading e-books. It is not at this writing a common practice or popular option with readers.

- The channels of sale and distribution are not well established. Most literary agents, for example, don't know who the e-book publishers are – or if they do, don't have much experience dealing with them. Publishers who do digital books are not as easy to find as the traditional publishers.

## BUYING BOOKS ON THE INTERNET: AMAZON.COM BARNESANDNOBLE.COM BIBLIOFIND.COM

Thanks largely to Amazon.com and Barnes & Noble, many readers have grown accustomed to buying books online. These are primarily regular printed books published by regular publishers. The only thing new is the idea of buying online instead of going to a bookstore or a mail order catalog.

The biggest retail Web sites for buying new books are **www.amazon.com** and **www.barnesandnoble.com**. For buying out of print, used, and rare books, try **www.bibliofind.com**. Bibliofind was recently purchased by Amazon. In addition, the Author's Guild sells out-of-print books for its members through its out-of-print online selling service, www.backinprint.com.

Books are selling briskly on the Internet. They are the third-most frequently purchased product online, after computer hardware and software. When *Monica's Story,* Andrew Morton's book about the Monica Lewinsky affair was published, barnesandnoble.com was selling the book at a rate of more than two copies every minute, according to the *Wall Street Journal* (March 5, 1999).

*The Strand*, New York City's most famous used bookstore, will search their "8 miles of books" for a particular title for you. Their phone number is (212) 473-1452. They do not have a Web site.

## INTERNET PRINT-ON-DEMAND

Print-on-demand isn't, strictly speaking, Internet publishing. But print-on-demand is often used in conjunction with online selling.

Print-on-demand allows a publisher to print small volumes of a book, or even print copies of a book one at a time as orders come in. Typically a customer goes to the Web site and orders a book. The book is then printed, bound, and shipped.

With this technology, authors can keep their books in print longer. Once the regular publisher has put the book out of print, it can be taken to an electronic publisher. The electronic publisher, for a fee, will offer your book for sale on the Internet and provide print-on-demand for fulfilling orders.

The Author's Guild out-of-print Web site, **www.backinprint.com**, now has print-on-demand capability. According to an article in *Publishers Weekly* (August 16, 1999), famous authors including Roger Angell and Judy Blume have already signed up for this service.

The new Internet tie-in with print-on-demand capability will give authors a cost-effective way to continue selling their book and have it available long after the regular publisher has put it out of print. You earn more income and extend the life of a work that's probably important to you. "Digital printing could let book publishers cut their stocks while keeping their whole backlist permanently available, by printing books only when retailers or individual customers ask for them," reports *The Economist* (January 1, 1999 and October 21, 1999). "Production and distribution costs are reduced to almost nothing when the 'book' is basically a computer file. Returns are eliminated."

Another advantage of print-on-demand technology is that

the books can be available faster than with the traditional book printing process. This can be important with a timely book or when racing against others to get a book out on a particularly newsy subject. Using print-on-demand technology, Pocket Books recently released an e-book version of one of their books (*Knockdown: The Harrowing True Account of a Yacht Race Turned Deadly*, by Martin Dugard) 6 weeks before the hardcover edition became available. The e-book could be printed on demand as a full-size softcover edition or downloaded digitally into a Rocket eBook reading device.

## IUNIVERSE: PRINT-ON-DEMAND/INTERNET PUBLISHER

The print-on-demand publishing for www.backinprint.com is being handled by toExcel, one of the early innovators in this field. Toexcel is a business unit of iUniverese.com, which – on its Web site, **www.iuniverse.com** – promotes itself as the "World's Largest Publishing Portal."

A portal is an entry point to a Web site or service that offers a broad array of resources and services, such as e-mail, forums, search engines, and on-line shopping malls. The first Web portals were online services, such as AOL, that provided access to the Web, but by now most of the traditional search engines have transformed themselves into Web portals to attract and keep a larger audience.

ToExcel and other Internet publishers offer services to both experienced and first-time authors. First-time authors can pay to have their book published (electronically or in small print-on-demand press runs) and sold via the publishers' Web sites. Experienced authors can find a home for books they couldn't or didn't want to sell to mainstream publishers, as well as give their out-of-print books a second life.

For example, first-time author Natasha Munson got her manuscript for *My Black Girls: How to Make Wise Choices and Live a Life You Love* published by iUniverse. "iUniverse is making my dream a reality by publishing my book and partnering with  Barnes & Noble stores nationwide this month," says Munson. "This has been an unbelievable experience and a breakthrough for my writing career."

I recently co-authored a book titled *Natural Alternatives to Viagra*. When the publisher, Carol Publishing, went out of business, my agent resold the book to iUniverse, and the book is due out in 2000.

"Our main intention is for people to buy the printed trade paperback but over the Internet," my editor at iUniverse, Dana Isaacson, explains. "Using on-demand technology cuts out the warehousing costs and makes for higher profitability, despite the high costs involved with on-demand printing. We feel we have an interesting and efficient business model, and that everyone will benefit."

Xerox is one of the major manufacturers of print-on-demand production technology for the digital book market.

## FATBRAIN: ONLINE PUBLISHING

Print-on-demand is one Internet marketing method. Another is true online publishing, where the book is not only sold on the Internet, but also delivered through it as an electronic file the buyer can download and print out.

One such site is **www.fatbrain.com**, which calls these online documents "eMatter." The eMatter doesn't have to be a regular book – it can be anything from a short booklet to a full-sized book. Interested readers can download your document to their PC using their credit card on the Fatbrain Web site. They can then read it online or print it out – no special equipment required.

You can post your document for a minimal fee of only one dollar a month. And you can charge any price you wish for it. In addition to the small posting fee, fatbrain.com takes the payment online. Then they split it 50-50 with you: If they collect $30 from someone who buys one copy of your book online, they will send you a check for $15.

According to an article in *Newsweek* (October, 1999), Fatbrain posts some 20,000 items from 2,800 authors. You can contact fatbrain at the **www.fatbrain.com** Web site or by calling toll-free 800-789-8590.

## ONLINE PUBLISHER: PUBLISHINGONLINE.COM

Publishing Online (**www.PublishingOnline.com**) bills itself as "the Internet's premier publishing house." The site posts books online that customers can download, for a fee, either to their PCs or to an e-book electronic reading device such as a Rocket Book or SoftBook. They also offer regular print copies of books through print-on-demand technology.

You can publish your e-book on PublishingOnline.com for a one-time set-up fee of only $49. If you have an out of print book that is not in electronic format, they will scan it for you and convert to the appropriate file format.

Publishing Online.com pays authors a 40 percent royalty fee for every book sold vs. the 7 to 15 percent royalty typical of regular publishers. You can price your book as you wish, but Publishing Online finds that e-books sell best when they're about half the price of regular bookstore books. You can also link your own Web site to PublishingOnline.com.

## NETBOOKS.COM

**Netbooks.com** is a Web site offering downloadable digital titles for sale. They also sell hard copies of books produced using print-on-demand technology.

Right now, Netbooks offers more than 200 titles on its Web site at **www.netbooks.com**. They plan to expand the offering to several thousand. Browsers can preview the book's text in a separate browser window before deciding whether to buy. Online purchase prices start at $2.95 per book.

## E-BOOK READING DEVICES.

Simply posting your book online and allowing readers to download to a PC, where they can read your book on screen or as a print out, is one e-publishing option.

Another is to post your e-book as a file that can be downloaded onto a special e-book electronic reading device. These are portable hand-held units that display the book on a screen in a format that looks much more like a page in a regular printed book than merely reading a text or Word file on a regular PC.

There are a variety of download formats for e-books including Adobe PDF, SoftBook e-reader, and HTML. Short documents can also be downloaded and read on a Palm Pilot.

Companies that are developing e-book readers or e-book technology include J-Stream, Nuvo Media, Softbook Press, Glassbook, Everybook, and Librius.

The best-selling reading devices seem to be the Softbook and Nuvo Media's Rocket eBook.

The Rocket eBook weighs only 22 ounces and can hold 41,000 pages of text and graphics – the equivalent of 200 full-size books. There are currently 2,000 titles you can download from various sources, including barnesandnoble.com, into a Rocket eBook reader.

The Rocket eBook reader sells for around $199. For more information, visit **www.rocket-ebook.com**. They are also on sale at many Barnes & Noble stores.

The other popular e-book reading device is the SoftBook system, from SoftBook Press. Similar to a Rocket eBook, the SoftBook system holds up to 65,000 pages of text and graphics. It features a large page display, a built-in modem, and Ethernet compatibility. For more information visit **www.softbook.com**.

Librius makes a well-received electronic reader called the Millennium Reader. It weighs only 10 ounces. "With these new e-books, the Internet is your bookstore," writes Suzanne Kantra Kirschner in *Popular Science* (February 1999). Kirschner says she likes e-books because she can read with one hand, paging through a book by pressing a button with her thumb. The back-lit display also allows reading in dim light – for instance, in a car at night, or in bed when your significant other is asleep.

Microsoft has gotten into the game with Microsoft Reader. Unlike the Rocket eBook and SoftBook, which are hardware, Microsoft Reader is software that displays electronic books on ordinary desktop and laptop PCs running Windows 95, Windows 98, or Windows NT.

One organization, the Open eBook authoring group, has announced final approval of a file specification for e-book publishing. The standard is known as Open eBook Publication Structure 1.0.

Based on Internet programming language HTML, Open eBook Publication Structure is designed to allow texts to be read on any electronic device: desktop PCs and laptops, e-book readers, Palm Pilots, and other hardware. For more information on the standard, visit **www.openbook.org**.

## ROSEDOG.COM

RoseDog.com is not an online publisher or e-book seller. As their ad in *Poets & Writers* magazine explains, "RoseDog is the newest Internet venue for emerging writers. We showcase as much of your work as you want." They claim to have a site "engineered to attract the people who count for you – agents and publishers."

There is no cost for aspiring writers to become members or post their work. Manuscripts are simply submitted as plain text attachments to an e-mail, and are posted within minutes of transmission.

The Web site, **www.rosedog.com**, gives detailed explanation of how to get your work on RoseDog and what the potential benefits may be. I did not find any evidence that participating has helped people sell their work to mainstream publishers, or that agents and publishers do indeed come to the site looking for promising material. If this is the case, I hope they add this information to the site.

Never before in history have there been as many options available to the writer aspiring to be a published book author. When you combine mainstream publishing with the print-on-demand and electronic publishing options made available by the latest technologies, the question is no longer, "can I get my book published?" but rather "how do I want to have my book published? The choice is yours.

I'd love to hear your experiences in getting your book published. The best way to contact me is by via e-mail: Rwbly@bly.com

Good luck!

# APPENDIX A

# DIRECTORY OF SELECTED BOOK PUBLISHERS

**Addison-Wesley Publishing Co.**
General Books Division
Route 128
One Jacob Way
Reading, MA  01867
617-944-3700

**AMACOM Books**
American Management Assn.
135 West 50th Street
New York, NY  10020
212-586-8100

**Andrews and McNeel**
4900 Main Street
Kansas City, MO  64112
816-932-6700

**Avon Books**
1350 Avenue of the Americas
New York, NY  10019
212-261-6800

**The Ballantine Publishing Group**
**Ballantine/Del Rey/Fawcett/Columbine/**
**House of Collectibles/Moorings/One World/Ivy Books**
201 East 50th Street
New York, NY  10022
212-751-2600

**Bantam Doubleday Dell Publishing Group**
1540 Broadway
New York, NY 10036
212-354-6500

**Barron's Educational Series Inc.**
250 Wireless Blvd.
Hauppauge, NY 11788
516-434-3311

**The Berkley Publishing Group**
200 Madison Avenue
New York, NY 10016
212-951-8800

**Career Press**
3 Tice Road
PO Box 687
Franklin Lakes, NJ 07417
201-848-0310

**Carroll & Graf Publishers**
260 Fifth Avenue
New York, NY 10001
212-889-8772

**Consumer Reports Books**
101 Truman Avenue
Yonkers, NY 10703
914-378-2000

**Contemporary Books**
2 Prudential Plaza
Suite 1200
Chicago, IL 60601
312-540-4500

**Crisp Publications**
1200 Hamilton Court
Menlo Park, CA  94025
415-949-4988

**The Dartnell Corporation**
4660 North Ravenswood Avenue
Chicago, IL  60640
312-561-4000

**Dearborn Publishing Group**
155 North Wacker Drive
Chicago, IL  60606
312-836-4400

**Donald I. Fine Inc.**
19 West 21st Street
Suite 402
New York, NY  10010
212-727-3270

**Facts On File**
460 Park Avenue South
New York, NY  10016
212-683-2244

**Farrar Straus Giroux**
19 Union Square West
New York, NY  10003
212-741-6900

**Fireside Books**
1230 Avenue of the Americas
New York, NY  10020
212-698-7000

**Gale**
835 Penobscot Building
Detroit, MI 48226
313-961-2242

**Grolier Inc.**
Franklin Watts
Orchard Books
95 Madison Avenue
New York, NY 10016
212-951-2650

**Gulf Publishing Company**
PO Box 2608
Houston, TX 77252
713-529-4301

**Harcourt Brace & Co.**
111 Fifth Avenue
New York, NY 10003
212-592-1000

**Harper Collins Publishers**
10 East 53rd Street
New York, NY 10022
212-207-7000

**Health Communications Inc.**
3201 Southwest 15th Street
Deerfield Beach, FL 33442
305-360-0909

**Henry Holt & Company**
115 West 18th Street
New York, NY 10011
212-886-9200

### Houghton Mifflin Co.
222 Berkeley Street
Boston, MA  02116-3764
617-725-5000

### Hyperion
114 Fifth Avenue
New York, NY  10011
212-633-4400

### IDG Books Worldwide
919 East Hillsdale Blvd.
Suite 400
Foster City, CA  94404
415-655-3000

### Irwin Professional Publishing
1333 Burr Ridge Road
Burr Ridge, IL  60521
708-789-4000

### John Wiley & Sons
605 Third Avenue
New York, NY  10158
212-850-6000

### Kensington Publishing Corporation
### Zebra Books/Pinnacle Books/Z-Fave
850 Third Avenue  16th Floor
New York, NY  10022
212-407-1500

### Kodansha America
Kodansha Intl.
114 Fifth Avenue
New York, NY  10011
212-727-6460

**Little, Brown & Company**
1271 Avenue of the Americas
New York, NY  10020
212-522-8700

**M. Evans & Co.**
216 East 49th Street
New York, NY  10017
212-688-2810

**MacMillan Publishing**
**MacMillan General Reference**
**MacMillan Consumer Information**
1633 Broadway
New York, NY  10019
212-654-1000

**McGraw-Publishing Group**
11 West 19th Street
New York, NY  10011
212-512-2000

**NTC Publishing Group**
**Passport Books**
**National Textbook Company**
4255 West Touhy Avenue
Lincolnwood, IL  60646
708-679-5500

**Penguin USA**
**Viking**
**Dutton**
375 Hudson Street
New York, NY  10014
212-366-2000

## Pocket Books
1230 Avenue of the Americas
New York, NY  10020
212-698-7000

## Prentice Hall Business,Training & Healthcare Group
## Prentice Hall Career & Personal Development
Prentice Hall Building
113 Sylvan Avenue Route 9W
Englewood Cliffs, NJ  07632
201-592-2000

## Price Stern Sloan
11150 Olympic Boulevard
Suite 650
Los Angeles, CA  90064
310-477-6100

## Prima Publishing
3875 Atherton Road
Rocklin, CA  95765
916-632-4400

## Prometheus Books
59 John Glenn Drive
Buffalo, NY  14228
716-837-2475

## Random House
## Ballantine Publishing Group/Crown Publishing Group
## Knopf Publishing Group/Pantheon/Schocken/Times Book
201 East 50th Street
New York, NY  10022
212-751-2600

## Reader's Digest General Books
260 Madison Avenue
New York, NY  10016
212-953-0030

**Regnery Publishing Inc.**
1130 17th Street NW
Suite 600
Washington, DC  20036
202-457-0978

**Rodale Press**
33 East Minor Street
Emmaus, PA  18098-0099
610-967-5171

**Scholastic Inc.**
730 Broadway
New York, NY  10003
212-343-6100

**Scribner**
1230 Avenue of the Americas
New York, NY  10020
212-698-7000

**Self-Counsel Press**
1704 North State Street
Bellingham, WA  98225
360-676-4530

**St. Martin's Press**
175 Fifth Avenue
New York, NY  10010
212-674-5151

**Stackpole Books**
5067 Ritter Road
Mechanicsburg, PA  17055
717-796-0411

**Sybex Inc.**
2021 Challenger Drive
Alameda, CA  94501
415-523-8233

**Ten Speed Press/Celestial Arts**
PO Box 7123
Berkeley, CA  94707
510-559-1600

**The Putnam Berkley Group**
200 Madison Avenue
New York, NY  10016
212-951-8400

**W. H. Freeman & Co.**
41 Madison Avenue
New York, NY  10010
212-576-9400

**W.W. Norton & Co.Inc.**
500 Fifth Avenue
New York, NY  10110
212-354-5500

**Warner Books**
Time & Life Building
1271 Avenue of the Americas
New York, NY  10020
212-522-7200

**William Morrow & Co.Inc.**
**Avon Books**
1350 Avenue of the Americas
New York, NY  10019
212-261-6500

**Workman Publishing Company**
708 Broadway
New York, NY 10003
212-254-5900

**Writer's Digest Books**
**North Light Books/Betterway Books/Story Press**
1507 Dana Avenue
Cincinnati, OH 45207
513-531-2222

**Ziff-Davis Press**
5903 Christie Avenue
Emeryville, CA 94608
510-601-2000

ADDITIONAL LISTINGS FOR PUBLISHERS MAY BE FOUND
IN THE FOLLOWING REFERENCE GUIDES:

*Insider's Guide to Book Editors, Publishers, and Literary Agents*
   by Jeff Herman
   Rocklin, CA: Prima Publishing

*LMP*
*Literary Market Place*
   New York, NY: R.R. Bowker
   Updated annually

*Writer's Market*
   Cincinnati, Ohio: Writer's Digest Books
   Updated annually

# APPENDIX B

# DIRECTORY OF SELECTED LITERARY AGENTS

**AEI**
**Atchity Editorial/Entertainment Intl.**
Literary Management and Production
9601 Wilshire Blvd. Suite 1202
Beverly Hills, CA 90210
213-932-0407

**Arthur Pine & Associates**
250 W. 57th Street, Suite 417
New York, NY 10019
212-265-7330

**Bill Gladstone**
Waterside Productions
2191 San Elijo Avenue
Cardiff-by-the-Sea, CA 92007
619-632-9190

**B.K. Nelson Literary Agency**
84 Woodland Rd.
Pleasantville, NY 10570
914-741-1322

**Carol Mann Literary Agency**
55 Fifth Avenue
New York, NY 10003
212-206-5635

**Connie Clausen & Associates Literary Agency**
250 East 87th Street
New York, NY  10128
212-427-6135

**Curtis Brown Ltd.**
10 Astor Place
New York, NY  10003
212-473-5400

**Denise Marcil Literary Agency Inc.**
685 West End Avenue, 9C
New York, NY  10025
212-932-3110

**Dominick Abel Literary Agency**
146 West 82nd Street  #1B
New York, NY 10024
212-877-0710

**Donald Maass Literary Agency**
157 West 57th Street
Suite 1003
New York, NY  10019
212-757-7755

**Ellen Levine Literary Agency**
15 East 26th Street
Suite 1801
New York, NY  10010
212-889-0620

**FIFI Oscard Agency Inc.**
24 West 40th Street
New York, NY  10018
212-764-1100

## Gerald McCauley Agency
PO Box 844
Katonah, NY  10536
914-232-5700

## Harold Schmidt Literary Agency
343 West 12th Street
Suite 1B
New York, NY  10014
212-727-7473

## Harvey Klinger Inc.
301 West 53rd Street
New York, NY  10019
212-581-7068

## Hull House Literary Agency
240 East 82nd Street
New York, NY  10028
212-988-0725

## Lisa Bankhoff
## ICM
40 West 57th Street
New York, NY 10019
212-556-5600

## Irene Goodman Literary Agency
521 Fifth Avenue
New York, NY  10175
212-682-1978

## John Hawkins & Associates
71 West 23rd Street Suite 1600
New York, NY  10010
212-807-7040

**Judith Riven Literary Agency**
250 West 16th Street 4F
New York, NY 10011
212-255-1009

**Kidde, Hoyt & Picard**
335 East 51st Street
New York, NY 10022
212-755-9461

**Literary Group**
270 Lafayette Street, Suite 1505
New York, NY 10012
212-274-1616

**L. Perkins Associates**
5800 Arlington Avenue
Suite 18J
Riverdale, NY 10471
212-304-1607

**Lowenstein Associates**
121 West 27th Street
Suite 601
New York, NY 10001
212-206-1630

**Max Gartenberg Literary Agency**
521 Fifth Avenue Suite 1700
New York, NY 10175
212-860-8451

**McIntosh and Otis Inc.**
310 Madison Avenue
New York, NY 10017
212-687-7400

**Meredith Bernstein Literary Agency Inc.**
2112 Broadway  Suite 503A
New York, NY  10023
212-799-1007

**Michael Carlisle**
Carlisle & Company
24 East 64th Street
New York, NY 10021
212-813-1881

**Michael Larsen/Elizabeth Pomada Literary Agency**
1029 Jones Street
San Francisco, CA  94109
415-673-0939

**Miriam Altshuler Literary Agency**
RR 1 Box 5
Old Post Road
Red Hook, NY  12571
914-758-9408

**Philip G Spitzer Literary Agency**
50 Talmadge Farm Lane
Easthampton, NY  11937
516-329-3651

**PMA Literary and Film Management Inc.**
220 West 19th Street  Suite 501
New York, NY  10011
212-929-1222

**Raines & Raines**
71 Park Avenue
New York, NY  10016
212-684-5160

**Richard Curtis Associates Inc.**
171 East 24th Street
New York, NY  10021
212-772-7363

**Russell & Volkening Inc.**
50 West 29th Street #7E
New York, NY  10001
212-684-6050

**Ruth Nathan Literary Agency**
80 Fifth Avenue
Room 706
New York, NY  10011
212-675-6063

**Ruth Wreschner, Authors' Representative**
10 West 74th Street
New York, NY  10023-2304
212-877-2605

**Sandra Dukstra Literary Agency**
1155 Camino del Mar
Suite 515
Del Mar, CA  92014
619-755-3115

**Faith Hamlin**
**Sanford J. Greenburg Associations**
55 Fifth Avenue  15th Floor
New York, NY 10003
(212) 206-5607

**Scott Waxman**
**Scott Waxman Agency**
1650 Broadway #1101
New York, NY 10019
212-262-2388

**Shana Cohen**
**Stuart Kershevsky Agency**
381 Park Avenue South  Suite 819
New York, NY 10016
212-725-5288

**Stepping Stone Literary Agency**
59 West 71st Street
Suite 9B
New York, NY  10023
212-362-9277

**Susan & Protter Literary Agency**
110 West 40th Street #1408
New York, NY  10018
212-840-0480

**Tony Seidl**
**TD Media**
300 E. 59th Street  #176
New York, NY 10022
(212) 588-0807

**The Fogelman Literary Agency**
7515 Greenville Avenue
Suite 712
Dallas, TX  75231
214-361-9956

**The Jeff Herman Agency Inc.**
500 Greenwich Street
Suite 501C
New York, NY  10013
212-941-0540

**The Richard Parks Agency**
138 East 16th Street
Suite 5B
New York, NY 10003
212-254-9067

**The Wendy Becker Literary Agency**
530-F Grand Street Suite 11-H
New York, NY 10002
212-228-5940

**Tim Hays Literary Agency**
923 Saw Mill River Road #147
Ardsley, NY 10502
(914) 478-5110

**Victoria Sanders Literary Agency**
241 Avenue of the Americas
Suite 11H
New York, NY 10014
212-633-8811

**Waterside Productions**
2191 San Elijo Aveenue
Cardiff-by-the-sea, CA 92007-1839
(619) 632-9190

**William Morris Agency Inc.**
1350 Avenue of the Americas
New York, NY 10019
212-903-1147

**Writers House**
21 West 26th Street
New York, NY 10010
212-685-2400

YOU CAN ALSO WRITE TO THESE PROFESSIONAL
SOCIETIES OF LITERARY AGENTS:

## Association of Author's Representatives
10 Astor Place, 3rd floor
New York, NY 10003
(212) 252-3695

## Literary Agents of North America
Author Aid Associates
340 E. 52nd Street
New York, NY 10022
(212) 759-4213

TRADE MAGAZINES ALSO ARE A GOOD RESOURCE FOR LEARNING
ABOUT AGENTS AND THE TYPE OF BOOKS THEY REPRESENT:

*Publisher's Weekly*
New York, NY
(800) 278-2991

*The Writer*
Boston, MA
(617) 423-3157

*Writer's Digest*
F&W Publications
Cincinnati, OH
(513) 531-2690

# APPENDIX C

# STANDARD PERMISSION FORM

If you intend to lift significant amounts of material from other sources and place it in your book, you should send a permission form, such as the one reprinted here, to the individual or firm owning the copyright to that material.

For material taken from self-published books and monographs, send the permission form to the author. For using text in books from regular publishers, send the form to the publishing house, attention of "Permissions Editor." For reprinting copy from magazine articles, write to the magazine in care of the "Permissions Editor" or "Managing Editor."

Copyright laws are open to interpretation, and we cannot give you strict guidelines on what is permissible in terms of copying material from other sources and what is not. The best advice is: Ask an attorney. If you have a book contract, ask your publisher for advice (they may also have their own permission form they want you to use).

As a rule of thumb, send a permission form whenever taking 50 words or more from a magazine article or 300 words or more from a book. When in doubt, send a permission form, and don't use the material until a signed permission form is returned to you by the copyright holder.

Just fill in the blanks as indicated on the form. Send the copyright holder an original plus one copy for their files. Include an SASE (self addressed stamped envelope) for return of one copy of the signed form to you. Keep permission forms on file permanently, so you can show proof that you obtained permission if a question arises later on.

Date_____

To:

From:

I am preparing a manuscript to be published by _____

Author/tentative title _____

Estimated publication date_____Approximate number of pages_____

I request your permission to include the following material in this and all subsequent editions of my book including versions made by nonprofit organizations for use of blind or physically handicapped persons, and in all foreign-language translations and other derivative works published or prepared by the publisher or its licensees, for distribution throughout the world.

Author(s) and/or editor(s) _____

Title of book or periodical _____

Title of selection_____Copyright date _____

from page_____, line_____, beginning with the words _____

from page_____, line_____, ending with the words _____

Figure #_____, on page_____Table,_____, on page _____

*(if necessary, attach continuation sheets)*

Please indicate agreement by signing and returning the enclosed copy of this letter. In signing, you warrant that you are the sole owner of the rights granted and that your material does not infringe upon the copyright or other rights of anyone. If you do not control these rights, I would appreciate your letting me know to whom I should apply.

Thank you.

_____

*Name*

Agreed to and accepted:

by _____

*Signature*　　　　　　　　*Title*　　*Date*

Credit and/or copyright notice: _____

# APPENDIX D

# SAMPLE BOOK PROPOSAL

Here is the proposal I wrote for my book, *Selling Your Services*, published in hardcover and paperback by Henry Holt & Company, a New York publishing firm.

BOOK PROPOSAL

SELLING YOUR SERVICES *Book title*

Proven strategies for getting clients to hire you
(or your firm) *Subtitle*

a guide for:
* consultants
* freelancers
* independent professionals
* contractors and vendors
* service firms
* and anyone else who works in a service or service related business

by Robert W. Bly
174 Holland Avenue
New Milford
(201) 599-2277

November 16, 1989

*Repeat title, subtitle and byline here*

SELLING YOUR SERVICES
Proven strategies for getting clients to
hire you (or your firm)
by Robert W. Bly

*Overview*

There are dozens of books on selling, but these books focus on selling products-physical, tangible items-and aimed at professional salespeople working on commission.

But there has never been a book on selling services which is as different from selling products as night is

184

from day.

Now *Selling Your Services* fills that gap, providing the hundreds of thousands of people in the service sector with proven strategies on how to sell.

*Differentiate yourself from the competition*

### Why A Book On Selling Services?

Selling services-which are intangibles-is fundamentally different and requires an entirely separate strategy from selling products-which are tangible. Among these key differences:

*This is a real attention-grabber...*
*note the 2 column format for easy reading.*

| Selling Products | Selling Services |
|---|---|
| Sold by professional salespeople who don't see the buyer once the sale is made and whose only concern is bringing back an order. | Frequently sold by the person who will actually render the service. This person must build a personal relationship with the buyer and has to select prospects with good personal chemistry; otherwise, the relationship will fail. |
| Sale is finished once the order is taken and product is delivered. | Getting a signed contract is only the first step. The client must be continuously sold and resold before, during, and after service is performed. |
| Proof of satisfaction is easy to demonstrate and is achieved when product is delivered. Salespeople, therefore, are not selective and will sell to basically anybody with money to buy. | Satisfaction is subjective. Therefore, service sellers must be sure to screen prospects and select only those prospects who seem a good fit with the sellers personnel and type of service. |
| Prospects are qualified by whether they have the money and authority to buy. | Prospects are qualified by whether their specific problems can be solved in a satisfactory manner by the service offered. |

Salesperson is primarily concerned with closing the sale and does not worry about whether the prospect will become a difficult account because salespeople do not have to personally deal with customer complaints (in most cases).

Salespeople will not pursue a sale to a difficult prospect when the salesperson is also the one who will have to cope with this person while rendering service.

Pricing is fairly standard and easy to calculate.

Pricing differs with each client and project and frequently requires intensive up-front effort in order to prepare a quotation or proposal.

Visits from salespeople are always free.

Some service providers view visits and preparation of bids or proposals as consulting work and may want to charge for the services (e.g., lawyers who charge a small initial consultation fee to listen and decide whether to take your case).

Salespeople use volume discounts and price bargaining as a prime negotiations tool for closing sales.

Prices not greatly flexible because service business is labor-intensive and firm cannot lose money on initial contract in exchange for promise of future business as is often done in product selling.

Salesperson is viewed by prospect as a salesman and is not expected to be an expert.

Salesperson is viewed by prospect as a consultant and the prospects image of the service firm is dependent largely upon how well this consultant performs in initial meetings.

Salesperson is paid commission, creating a powerful incentive to sell as much product as possible.

Salesperson must also render services sold (or at least part of them), so they may be hesitant to sell more than he or she can handle.

*This list shows the editor that there is a clear difference in my book vs. others*

Product salespeople are trained to overcome objections and sell the prospect despite his protestations that he does not want to buy.

In service selling, an objection is not necessarily something to be overcome but, rather, serves as a warning signal that the person might be a bad match for your service and that the meeting should be ended.

Customer is buying an off-the-shelf item which is mass-produced and not tailored to his specific needs.

Customer is buying (and expects to get) a service that is highly customized and tailored to his specific needs.

*Overview continues...*

Today America has made the transition from a product-producing to a service-providing economy. According to a recent article in Executive Business Magazine, 35 percent of the U.S. work force was employed in manufacturing in 1970. That figure grew to 60 percent in 1987. The U.S. Bureau of labor statistics reports that approximately 21 million Americans were employed in manufacturing versus nearly 36 million in service businesses in 1987, the most recent year for which accurate figures are available.

*Note use of statistics to add credibitlity*

Because of this shift from a manufacturing to a service economy, most books on selling which focus on goods rather than services, information, or ideas-are not applicable in today's sales environment.

Furthermore, even manufacturing companies are becoming service sellers. As buyers see less and less difference between manufactured products, the factor that most influences their choice of vendor is service. Selling service has now become both a profit-center in its own right (IBM, for example, is one of hundreds of manufacturers that derived substantial income from service) as well as an integral component of any hard-good product. So everyone, even salespeople who traditionally think of themselves as "merchandise movers", is in fact a "service seller". The ability to provide and sell service is now critical to the success of every corporation, small business, and self-employed entrepreneur in the United States.

## MARKETS

*Selling Your Services* speaks directly to the needs of a number of large and easily identified target markets, both entrepreneurial and corporate:

1. Consultants.  Among self-employed professionals selling services, consultants are the most active and aggressive when it comes to sales and marketing; thus they will welcome a book that deals specifically with selling service  (which consultants render)  rather than product.  *Selling Your Services* will have great appeal to the more than 100,000 current and would-be independent consultants who eagerly purchase such books as Herman Holtz's, *How to Succeed as an Independent Consultant* (John Wiley; sales over 100,000 copies).

← *Note how I have demonstrated a large market with specific numbers*

2. Entrepreneur and  would-be entrepreneur. Because a service business can be started inexpensively in one's home or apartment, most of the 625,000 small businesses started each year are service businesses rather than manufacturing firms or distributors.  This book would have strong appeal to both working entrepreneur as well as those thinking about starting a business, i.e., readers of such publications as Inc. (Circulation: 600,000), *Entrepreneur* (circulation:  200,000), and *Nations Business* (850,000). Dr. Jeffrey Lant, publisher of the Sure-Fire Business Success catalog, has a list of 75,000 such people who are proven buyers of books on entrepreneurial topics.

3. Service and service-related firms. Perhaps the strongest market is the individual entrepreneur, small firms, and medium to large-size corporations that derive all or part of their income from selling services. This is the only book that presents proven strategies for getting people to buy services rather than products.

Dozens of industries and types of businesses and professions fall into this category including:

Accountants
Ad Agencies
Architects
Attorneies
Automobile
Banks And Financial Services Institutions
Barbers
Builders, Contractors, Remodelers
Bed And Breakfast Inns
Business And Management Consultants
Camps
Career Training Firms
Child Care, Baby Setting,  Pre-School Centers
Computer Programmers, Custom Software Developers, DP Consultants

Contractors
Construction Firms
Dating Services
Diaper Services
Dentists
Doctors
Dry Cleaning And  Laundry Establishments
Editorial Services
Electronics Repair Shops
Engineering And Consulting Engineer Services
Environmental Testing Services
Event Planners
Executive Search Firms
Financial Planners
Franchise Owners
Freight Forwarders
Fund Raising Consultants
Funeral Parlors, Morticians
Graphics Artist
Hair And Beauty Parlors
Health Spa's And Exercise Clubs
Hospitals And Clinics
Hotels, Whatever To, Clubs, Restaurants
Insurance Agents
Interior Decorative, Design, Planning Services
Investment Agents
Maintenance And Service Firms
Metal Working And Fabrication Services
Musicians And Entertainment
Pharmacists
Photographers
Proofreaders
Psychiatrists And Psychologists (Therapists)
Real Estate Agents
Sewer And Drain Cleaning Services
Speakers
Stock Brokers
Tanning Salons
Tax Preparers
Telephone And Telecommunications Services
Training And Development Consultants
Temporary Employment Services
Transportation Firms
Travel Agents
Utilities
Veterinarians
Video Tape Rental Stores
Watch And Jewelry Repair Services
Wedding Consultants
Word Processing Services
Writers
X.-Ray, Ultrasound, NMR, Diagnostic Services.

*This list makes the editor think, "Wow, there is a big demand for this book!!"*

This is just a sampling; obviously, the list could be much, much longer.

## More markets ↓

4. Self-employed professionals. This group includes graphic artists, photographers, writers, copy writers, publicists, proof readers, secretarial services, attorneys, dentists, doctors, accountants, and other white-collar workers who are self-employed and must market and sell their professional services. Most are involved in advising, consulting, or rendering professional services from home offices equipped with computers, modem, and fax machines. The finished product is frequently in the form of a written report or other printed material.

5. Blue-collar entrepreneur. This group includes handymen, wall paperers, painters, plumbers, locksmiths, landscape architects, lawn maintenance workers, roofers, carpenters and other trades people who provide a variety of services, usually related to home repair and maintenance, to the local community. Most work within a 50-mile radius and run the business from a home office and hang pick-up truck or van.

### MARKETING AND PROMOTION

The most cost-effective way of promoting *Selling Your Services* is through the magazines in the selling field as well as the magazines and newsletters that reach prospective readers in specific vertical industries and professions (e.g., veterinarians, attorneys, dentists, doctors, consultants, freelance writers, graphic artists, photographers). A press release can inexpensively be sent to these publications, while copies could be targeted to those most likely to run a review or articles (these would be the selling magazines as well as magazines and newsletters that focus on marketing and selling in specific vertical industries, e.g., Cam Foote's *Creative Business* for freelance advertising writers and artists, or Howard Shenson's newsletter on marketing and selling consulting services). I can provide a list with the addresses and editors of most of the worthwhile publications.

Although the market is flooded with books on selling, *Selling Your Services* focuses on selling service instead of a product. Therefore, it has a better chance of standing out from the crowd and is more likely to be of interest to program directors and editors-especially those whose publications deal with a service field. One technique might be to write short articles tailored toward specific industries

and send them to these editors in exchange for a short
blurb promoting the book I would be happy to provide as
many of these articles as needed.

   Although the paperback would probably be too inexpensive to promote via stand-alone direct mail, there are
several widely distributed catalogs of business books for
which *Selling Your Services* would be a good selection.  We
could also test a postcard deck aimed at entrepreneurs,
especially a higher-priced hardcover version.  In addition,
my survey of area book stores shows that selling is a
healthy category with many titles displayed; thus, *Selling
Your Services* could do well in bookstores. And it should be
slightly easier to sell to book store owners and buyers
because it's not just another sales book but, rather, has a
unique angle (i.e., it is a book about selling services,
not products or goods).

### COMPETITION

   There are over a hundred books listed in Books In Print on
topics of selling and sales.  But our book does not compete
with most of them, because it deals with selling services rather
than merchandise. So for our competitive analysis I eliminated:

*This*
*eliminates*  * books published before 1980
*the need*   * books self-published or published by small
*to*            or unknown presses
*research*   * books that are unavailable in book stores
*and*           and sold solely through direct mail
*describe*   * books on general selling that focused early
*books that*    or solely on traditional selling (i.e.,
*really do*     selling tangible items-goods, products,
*not*           merchandise)
*compete*    * books that focused on marketing only in an
*with mine.*    extremely narrow vertical market (e.g., a
                book on marketing only office products).

This leaves us with the following books as primary competion:
Minding other People's Business:  Winning Big for Your
Clients and Yourself by Donald L. Dell (New York: Villard
Books, 1989), 237 pp., hardcover, $18.95

   Although this is an excellent book, it is mostly
about dealing with and servicing clients rather than
selling.  Of its eight chapters, seven deal with client
service, client relations, and client contact.  Only one
chapter - Chapter Two: Getting Clients-deals with selling

or marketing services, and this chapter is 31 pages of
the book's 237 pages.

**Note how specific I am in researching competition.**

In addition, the book has two major flaws: first, almost all the stories and examples deal with sports management and marketing, which is the author's field (his company ProServ, represents 250 professional athletes). Second, the constant name-dropping celebrities in sports and
other fields eventually turns off the average reader, whose
business operates on a scale less grand.

By comparison, *Selling Your Services* is primarily about
selling and marketing to get new clients, rather than
servicing those clients you already have (although part of
my table of contents deals with this very important topic
of serving the client to ensure satisfaction and more
business after the initial sale is made). Also, I draw
examples from a wide range of fields, because as a consultant and teacher I have worked with firms in dozens of
industries.

2.  Marketing Your Consulting and Professional Services
Jeffrey P. Stone Davidson and Richard A. Conner (New
York: John Wiley & Sons, 1985), 219 pp, hardcover, $22.95.
This is a good book but too theoretical. It provides excellent coverage of marketing (e.g., creating a marketing
plan, identifying lists of prospects, classifying prospects
into categories, types of promotional vehicles available to
reach prospects) but does not provide adequate instruction
on selling, i.e., how to deal with and sell prospects over
the telephone or in face-to-face meetings. For example, of
the book's 219 pages, only one 16-page chapter (Chapter 9),
is devoted to personal selling.

*Selling Your Services*, by comparison, tells you what to
say and when to say it in order to get the prospect to hire
you. Actual dialogue the reader can adapt to his or her
own situation will enable the reader to overcome  virtually
every objection he or she might hear, from "I already use
someone else" to "we don't need any right now" to "your
price is too high." Just as important, I will also tell
when not to push a prospect to buy your service. Knowing
how to solicit the right clients is as critical to success
in any service industry as knowing how to overcome objections and close the sale.

**Identify competitor's _flaws_ and show
how YOUR book is better!**

## FORMAT

*Selling Your Services* is organized to reflect the precise sequence of things the reader must do to success-fully sell his or her services to the client – from gener-ating a sales lead and making the initial contacts, to making the presentation, preparing the price quotation , and getting a signed contract.

The book is divided into five major sections and 16 chapters.  I see *Selling Your Professional Services* as a medium-length, conversational, accessible guide rather than a treatise – a trade paperback (and possibly hardcover, for corporate and library sales) of approximately 200 pages. Target length would be between 65,000 and 75,000 words.

*Word length of the book*

Although the book would be mostly straight text, there would be some graphics, consisting mainly of sample materi-als the reader could copy and use in his or her daily selling work.  These would include sample contracts, pro-posals, price quotation, letters of agreement, telephone scripts, sales letters, promotional brochures, ads, press releases, and other marketing documents.

*Visuals, examples, and samples are selling points.*

**SELLING YOUR SERVICES: TABLE OF CONTENTS**

*Content outline of your proposed book*

**Introduction**

PART I: SOLID-GOLD PROSPECTING: HOW TO GENERATE INITIAL INTEREST IN YOUR SERVICES

**Chapter 1: *Selling Your Services*: an overview**

Selling services vs. selling products: similarities and differences.
The three-part service marketing strategy: inquiry genera-tion/direct response marketing, visibility/credibility-building, and inquiry fulfillment/marketing support. Sell-ing services to consumers. Selling services to business.

**Chapter 2: Sales lead-generating techniques that work**
Inquiry generation/direct-response marketing techniques that work: sales letters, direct mail, telemarketing, cold

calling, self-mailers, postcard decks, referrals, personal selling.

**Chapter 3: How to become famous in your field**
Gaining visibility and establishing credibility: articles, media coverage, books, speeches, seminars, professional groups, trade associations, presentations, publicity, monographs, special reports, networking, teaching.

**Chapter 4: How to create marketing documents that sell.**
Inquiry/marketing support materials: capabilities brochures, service-specific brochures, sales kits and folders, overhead and slide presentations, videotapes, audio cassettes, booklets, bios, resumes, business cards flyers.

**PART II: FOLLOW-UP: HOW TO GET APPOINTMENTS WITH PROSPECTS**

**Chapter 5: Proven techniques for prequalifing your prospects**
Follow-up techniques that presell your prospect, identify areas of need, and screen out non-prospects. Ranking prospects. Tracking sales activities.

**Chapter 6: How to get your prospects to talk with you**
Phone and mail strategies for getting past the secretary barrier.

**Chapter 7: Getting the initial appointment**
How to sell the meeting to your prospect in 30 seconds or less.

**Part III: THE ADDITIONAL CLIENT MEETING: HOW TO USE IT TO ACHIEVE YOUR GOAL.**

**Chapter 8: Increasing your selling efficiency**
The initial meeting - fee or free? How to decide when to meet with clients gratis-and when to charge for initial meetings. Plus: strategies to get clients to hire you by mail.

**Chapter 9: Consultative selling**
Why prospects want consultants, not salesmen. Why you should use the initial meeting to solve the client's problem, not sell.

**Chapter 10: How to handle objections**
Objections: How to use them as screening devices to eliminate potential problem clients and concentrate on your best prospects. How to answer agenda questions and client concerns.

**Chapter 11: Closing the sale**
How to move the client to the next step – a signed con-
tract-in the shortest possible period of time.

**PART IV.: GETTING THE PROJECT CONTRACTS, PROPOSALS, AND
LETTERS OF AGREEMENT**

**Chapter 12: How to ask for-and get-the fee you deserve**
Price quotation: how to set and get your fees.

**Chapter 13: The written agreement**
How to put it in writing with: contracts, proposals, and
letters of agreement.

**PART V.: CONTINUOUS SELLING: HOW TO KEEP CLIENTS SOLD AFTER
THE SALE IS MADE**

**Chapter 14: How to increase your sales with client satis-
faction.**
Tips on performing your service so the client is satisfied.

**Chapter 15: Coping with difficult clients.**
How to spot and correct problems before they harm your
client relationship

**Chapter 16: The key to successful service selling.**
The key: don't give your client his money's worth-give him
more than his money's worth.  This chapter outlines the
little (but important) things you can do to make the client
love you.

*Your "expert credentials in the subject matter of this book*

**ABOUT THE AUTHOR**

   In his work as an independent marketing consultant,
copywriter, and seminar leader, Bob Bly has helped dozens
of companies and hundreds of individuals sell more of their
professional and  consulting services through his articles,
lectures and training sessions.

   In addition, he has written sales letters, direct response ads, brochures, and other marketing documents that
have generated millions of dollars in sales for such ser-
vice-business clients as Value Rent-A-Car, Midlantic National Bank, American Medical Collection Agency, Advantage
Presort Service, JMW Consultants, Medrecon, and Fala Direct

Marketing. His service-industry clients are in a variety of businesses ranging from car rentals, consulting, and data processing to mail presorting, collection agencies, and P.R. Firms.

Bob Bly is the author of 17 books including *How to Promote Your Own Business* (New American Library), *Create The Perfect Sales Piece: How To Produce Brochures, Catalog, Fliers, And Pamphlets* (John Wiley & sons), and *The Copywriter's Handbook: A Step-by-step Guide To Writing Copy That Sales* and *Secrets Of A Freelance Writer: How To Make $85,000 A Year* (originally Dodd, Mead; New Edition to be published by Henry Holt). *Writing credentials*

Bob writes a regular column for *Direct Marketing* magazine and has been published in *Business Marketing, Executive Business, Amtrak Express, Writer's Digest, New Jersey Monthly,* and *Cosmopolitan.*

# APPENDIX E

# SAMPLE BOOK CONTRACT

Here is the Henry Holt contract for *Selling Your Services*, the book outlined in the book proposal in Appendix D. We've annotated it with some comments explaining the terms and conditions in the various clauses.

# HENRY HOLT AND COMPANY INC.

115 West 18th Street, New York, NY 10011  Tel (212)886-9200

## *Sample book contract*

AGREEMENT made this **21st** day of **March, 1990**, between Henry
Holt and Company, Inc., 115 West 18th Street, New York, N.Y.
10011 ("the "Publisher") and **Robert W. Bly**

**c/o Dominick Abel Literary Agency, Inc.**

**146 W. 82nd Street**

**New York, N.Y. 10024**

(the "Author") with respect to a book tentatively entitled

*Selling Your Services*_____(the "Work").

**1. GRANT OF RIGHTS** *You are only selling rights in U.S. and North America, **not** world rights*

Author grants to Publisher the exclusive right to print,
publish, distribute and sell the Work and to exercise the
subsidiary rights listed in paragraph 5 below in **the United
States of America, its possessions, the Philippine Republic
and the Dominion of Canada, All territories outside the United
States of America, its possessions, the Philippine Republic
and the Dominion of Canada and the British Commonwealth shall
be considered an Open Market for all copies of the Work.**

(the "Territory") Except as otherwise provided herein. Publisher may exercise the rights granted for the full term of
copyright (including any renewals and extensions) provided by
law in each country included within the Territory, under any
copyright laws now or hereafter in force.

**2. THE WORK**                        *topic of the book*

**a)** The Work is described as follows: A Guide to "*Selling Your
Services*" in America's service-orientated economy.

Of not less than **65,000** words,        *length of manuscript*

and not more than **75,000** words.

1

**b)** Except as otherwise disclosed by Author in writing to Publisher prior to the execution of this Agreement, Author agrees that the Work will be Author's next work. Author will deliver to Publisher on or before

_____ **January 1, 1991** _____ *due date - about 9 months*
_____ *from signing of contract*

("Due Date"), time being of the essence, two clean, typed, numbered, double spaced copies of the manuscript of the Work, all in form and content satisfactory to Publisher and complete and ready for the copyeditor, along with all illustrations, photographs, charts and any other necessary material, all in a form suitable for reproduction. Author will submit with manuscript on or before the Due Date all necessary permissions, releases, licenses and consents. Publisher shall have the right to have an index prepared at Author's expense, **and charged to his royalty account.**
*You pay for the preparation of the index*

**c) (i)** If Author does not deliver the complete manuscript of the Work to Publisher within thirty (30) days after the Due Date, or at another date as may have been agreed to by Publisher in writing, then upon Publisher's written notification thereof Author will repay to Publisher all amounts paid to Author under this Agreement. If the Work is delivered but deemed unsatisfactory, then upon Publisher's written notification thereof Author will repay to Publisher all amounts paid to Author under this Agreement. Upon repayment in full, Publisher will return to Author all rights granted herein.

*this is the killer; they can reject the book by saying it is "unsatisfactory"*

**(ii)** If Author fails to repay Publisher in full, all sums paid to or for the benefit of Author under this Agreement, then Publisher may, in addition to its other remedies, retain for its own account monies due Author under the terms of any other agreements between Author and Publisher until the amounts so retained equal the amount owing to Publisher.

**d)** If Publisher decides to submit the manuscript of the Work for legal, medical or other professional review, then the Work shall not be deemed complete and satisfactory unless all changes which may be requested by Publisher as the result of such review have been made by Author, regardless of whether or not any advance payment otherwise due to Author on delivery and acceptance of the manuscript has been made. Nothing contained in this paragraph will alter or vary any of the parties' rights under paragraph 15 of this Agreement.

## 3. ADVANCE

Publisher shall pay to Author as an advance against all monies accruing to Author under this Agreement the sum of _____ **Twelve Thousand five Hundred Dollars ($12,500)** _____ which shall be paid as follows:

**$6,250.00 on signature hereof:**    *Advance against royalties*

**$6,250.00 on delivery and acceptance of a complete and satisfactory manuscript for the Work, in conformity with paragraph 2 hereof.**

*The publisher has the right to*
2 *refuse to pay if they judge the work unsatisfactory!*

4. BOOK ROYALTIES

Publisher will pay to Author the following amounts:

a} Domestic

(i) **Hardcover**    *Hardcover royalty 10%–15%*
On all copies, less returns, of a regular trade hardcover edition (and revisions thereof) sold by Publisher in the United
States through normal trade channels (except as hereinafter set
forth}, the following royalties: **10% of the Publisher's invoice
price on the first 5,000 copies of the Work sold; 12.5% of the
invoice price on the next 5,000 copies sold; and 15% of the
invoice price on all copies sold thereafter.**

provided, however, that where the discount to booksellers is
fifty-five percent (55%) or more from the suggested list price,
the royalty shall be ten percent (10%) of net receipts.

(ii) **Paperback**
On all copies, less returns, of a paperback edition, sold
by Publisher in the United States through normal trade
channels (except as hereinafter set forth), a royalty of:
7.5% of the invoice price on all copies sold.

*Paperback royalty 7 1/2%*

(iii) **Unbound Sheets**
On sales of sheets of the Work, ten percent (10%) of the
amounts actually received by Publisher from such sales.

(iv) **Special Sales**
On all copies, less returns, of a regular hardcover or
paperback edition sold by Publisher outside normal wholesale and retail trade channels in the United States, ten
percent (10%) of the amounts actually received.

b) **Export**
On all copies, less returns, of a regular trade hardcover edition
or paperback edition of the Work sold by Publisher outside the
United States, an amount equal to ten percent (10%) of the amounts
actually received by Publisher in the United States.

c) **Premium**
On all copies of the Work sold by Publisher for premium use,
and on all copies sold of an edition specifically manufactured
for another party, Publisher shall pay five percent (5%) of the
amounts actually received by Publisher in the United States.

d) **Direct Marketing**
On all copies, less returns, of the Work sold by Publisher
directly to consumers as distinct from sales made to bookstores or wholesalers, five percent (5%) of the amounts actually received by Publisher.    *5% royalty on mail order sales*

e) **Promotions**
On all copies of the Work given away or sold at or below
Publisher's cost to promote the sale of the Work, no royalty
shall be paid.

3

## f) Special Printings

1  2 months or more after publication date, if in order to maintain the Work in print Publisher arranges for a printing two thousand (2,000) copies or less, then the royalties on all copies sold which were produced from such printing shall be one-half (1/2) of the royalty rates set forth in subparagraphs 4(a)(i) and 4(a)(ii). Publisher will not print in such small quantities more than twice in any year.

## g) Reduced Sales

If after the first two royalty accounting periods, sales during any period shall fall below five hundred (500) copies, the royalties on all the copies sold during such accounting period shall be one half (1/2) the royalty rates set forth on subparagraphs 4(a) (i) and 4(a) (ii).

## h) Freight Pass Through

It is understood and agreed that if Publisher uses a freight pass-through system while this Agreement is in effect, all royalties calculated on the basis of a suggested list price shall be calculated on the Gross Invoice price. The "Gross Invoice Price" shall mean the suggested list price less the freight pass-through increment. The freight pass-through (or jacket price) will not exceed the Gross Invoice Price by more than five percent (5%).

*Don't worry about freight pass through - your agent can explain it.*

## 5. SUBSIDIARY RIGHTS

a) The exclusive subsidiary rights referred to in paragraph 1 include all of the rights enumerated below. The amounts actually received by Publisher in the United States from the sales or license of such rights within the Territory are to be shared by Author and Publisher in the percentages indicated:

| | Author's Share | Publishers Share |
|---|---|---|
| (i) ~~First Serial~~<br>To ~~license~~ the work in whole or in part, ~~or in~~ a condensed or abridged version, ~~in~~ periodicals or newspapers, in one ~~or more~~ installments, ~~before publication in book form.~~ | 80% | 20% |

| | Author's Share | Publishers Share |
|---|---|---|
| (ii) Second Serial<br>To license the work in whole or in part, or in a condensed or abridged version, in periodicals or newspapers, in one or more installments, after publication in book form. | 50% | 50% |

| | ~~Author's Share~~ | ~~Publishers Share~~ |
|---|---|---|
| ~~(iii) English Language~~<br>~~To license English language rights in and to the work in book or serial form in full length, condensed or abridged versions for publication in countries outside the United States.~~ | 75% | 25% |

| | Author's Share | Publishers Share |
|---|---|---|
| ~~(iv) Translation~~<br>~~To license translation rights in and to the work in book or serial form in full length, condensed or abridged versions~~ | ~~50%~~ | ~~50%~~ |

| | Author's Share | Publishers Share |
|---|---|---|
| (v) Reprints<br>To license the Work to one or more publishers for reproduction in full-length, condensed or abridged versions in hardcover or paperbound reprint editions, including mass market, trade paperback or large-print edition's. | 50% | 50% |

*Author gets 50% of all income from article excerpts or reprints*

4

| **(vi) Permissions, Anthologies, Extracts, Abridged Versions, Collections** | **Author's Share** | **Publishers Share** |
|---|---|---|
| To license for publication excerpts, adaptations or abridgements of all or part of the Work. In addition, if the Publisher publishes the complete Work in a collection or anthology with one or more other works, Author shall be entitled to receive that proportion of the royalty payable under paragraph 4 which the Work bears to the total number of works contained in such collection. | 50% | 50% |

| **(vii) Book Club** | **Author's Share** | **Publishers Share** |
|---|---|---|
| To license the right to print, publish, and sell an edition of the Work to a book club or any organization which purchases book club rights, in full-length, condensed or abridged versions. | 50% | 50% |

Author gets only 50% of income from book club sales - this really hurt my income!

| ~~**(viii) Electronic Reproduction**~~ | ~~**Author's Share**~~ | ~~**Publishers Share**~~ |
|---|---|---|
| ~~To License reproduction of the work or parts of it by electronic, mechanical or any other form of copying, recording, or transmission now or hereafter known or devised, including, without limitation, copying, or by phonographic, photographic magnetic, or laser means onto film, microfiche, slides, filmstrips, transparencies, audio, and video cassette tapes, floppy disks, computer software media, or any other human or machine readable medium, and the broadcast or transmission thereof, but excluding all uses included in subparagraph 5(a) (ix). In addition, Publisher may exercise any of the aforementioned rights and pay the author a royalty of ten percent (10%) of the net amount received from such exercise.~~ | ~~50%~~ | ~~50%~~ |

| ~~**(ix) Motion Picture, Performance, Dramatization Rights**~~ | ~~**Author's Share**~~ | ~~**Publishers Share**~~ |
|---|---|---|
| ~~To license motion picture rights, radio rights, television rights, video cassette rights or the dramatic stage rights with or without music and public reading rights in connection with, the work.~~ | ~~75%~~ | ~~25%~~ |

| ~~**(x) Merchandising and Commercial Rights**~~ | ~~**Author's Share**~~ | ~~**Publishers Share**~~ |
|---|---|---|
| ~~To license merchandising and commercial rights in and to Author's name and the Work, subject to Author's approval which shall not be unreasonably withheld or delayed. Merchandising and commercial rights shall include, without limitation, the exploitation of the Work and of~~ | ~~50%~~ | ~~50%~~ |

~~Author's name in connection therewith,
and use of all material in the work,
including the characters contained
therein, through the use of the characters'
names or images and the simulation or
graphic exploitation thereof on or in
connection with the rights specified
in subparagraph 5(a) (ix), then the
royalties payable hereunder shall
be paid in the same proportion as
subparagraph 5(a) (ix). In addition,
Publisher may exercise any of the
aforementioned rights and pay the
author a royalty of ten percent (10%)
of the net amount received from such
exercise. Nothing herein shall be
construed to limit Publisher's
rights pursuant to paragraph 7 below.~~

b) **Promotional and Free Copies**
   Publisher may publish or permit others to publish or broadcast without
   charge and without royalty such selections from the Work for publicity
   purposes as may, in its opinion, benefit the sale of the Work. Publisher shall also be authorized to license publication of the Work
   without charge and without royalty in Braille or by any other method
   primarily designed for the physically or mentally handicapped.

c) All rights not specifically granted to Publisher herein are reserved
   for the Author for his exclusion use.

## 6. PUBLICATION

a) Within eighteen (18) months of its acceptance of the final manuscript
   and delivery of any other materials required pursuant to subparagraph
   2(b), Publisher will publish the Work at its own expense, in hardcover and/or in paperback in a style, manner, and at a price it deems
   best suited to the sale of the Work. It is understood that advertising, number and destination of free copies and all details of design,
   manufacture, distribution, marketing and promotion shall be at the
   discretion of Publisher. Publisher's failure to publish within such
   period shall not be deemed a breach of the Agreement if the delay is
   caused by any circumstances beyond its reasonable control.

   *Publisher must publish the book if they accept it or rights
   revert back to author (and author keeps the advance.)*

b) In the event Publisher shall fail to publish the Work within eighteen (18) months after Publisher's acceptance of the Work, Author
   may as his sole remedy at any time thereafter serve a written demand
   upon Publisher by registered mail, return receipt requested, requir-
   ing Publisher to publish the Work within ninety (90) days after
   receipt of such written demand, and if Publisher shall fail to
   comply with such demand within such ninety-day (90) day period, then
   this Agreement shall terminate without further notice at the end of
   such period, and all right, title and interest in and to the work
   shall revert to Author for his sole use and disposition. In the
   event of termination by the author pursuant to this paragraph, such
   payments as shall have been made to Author hereunder as advances
   shall be deemed in full discharge of all Publisher's obligations to
   Author pursuant to this Agreement and no other damages, claims,
   actions or proceedings, either legal equitable for breach of contract, default, failure to publish or otherwise, may be claimed,
   instituted, or maintained by Author against Publisher.

## 7. AUTHOR'S NAME

Publisher and its licensees may use Author's name, photograph and
likeness in the Work and in all revisions, editors, and versions
thereof and in connection with the work's advertising, promotion and
exercise of a rights granted to Publisher hereunder.

6

## 8.  COPYRIGHT

Publisher shall register the Work for copyright in the United States in the name of:_____ *Book is copyrighted by the*
_____ **Robert W. Bly**  *publisher in author's name*
If any part of the Work has been published and registered for copyright prior to January 1, 1978, Author: (i) agrees to timely apply for the renewer of the copyright prior to the expiration of the first term thereof, (ii) authorizes Publisher to take such application in the name of Author, and (iii) if this agreement has not been terminated previously, hereby assigns to Publisher the sole and exclusive right to print, publish and sell the work, and exercise the other rights referred to herein, during the full term of renewal and extensions of copyright, on the same terms and conditions as for the original copyright term.

## 9. REPORTS AND PAYMENTS

Statements of sales and earnings shall be made up semiannually to June thirtieth (30th) and December thirty-first (31st), and statements and settlement thereof in cash shall be made the following October twenty-fifth (25th) and April twenty-fifth (25th), respectively. Whenever the semiannual earnings fall below Twenty-Five Dollars ($25.00) no accounting or payment shall be made until the next settlement date after the earnings have aggregated Twenty Five Dollars ($25.00). Where any such statement indicates that Author has received an overpayment of royalties or is otherwise indebted to Publisher (individually and collectively, "Overpayment"), Publisher may deduct the amount of such Overpayment from any sums then or thereafter due Author from Publisher under this or any other agreement, it being understood and agreed that the term "Overpayment" excludes unearned advances except as may be specified in paragraph 3 hereinabove. If in Publisher's judgement there is risk of books sellers  returning unsold copies of the Work for credit, it may withhold for three accounting periods only a reasonable portion of Author's earned royalties for the purpose of adjusting Author's royalty account to make copies of the Work reported as sold represent firm sales.

## 10. AUTHOR'S CHANGES

Author agrees to read, revise, correct and return to Publisher first proof sheets of the Work within fourteen (14) days. Any expenses incurred by Publisher for Author's changes (other than corrections of printer's errors) which exceed ten percent (10%) of the total cost of composition shall be paid by Author.
*You pay for any extensive changes once the book has been typeset, so make your changes before that.*

## 11. REVISIONS

**a)** Author shall revise the first and subsequent editions of the Work when Author and publisher agree that such revision is necessary and supply any new matter necessary from time to time to keep the Work up to date, and on terms to be arranged. Author shall neglect or be unable to revise or supply new matter at a time and in form and content satisfactory to Publisher then Publisher shall have the right to engage some other person(s) to do so. When such revisions are not made by Author' Publisher shall cause such fact to be evidenced in the revised edition. Publisher shall have all rights in connection with all subsequent editions which Publisher has in the original Work.

**b)** All royalties to Author on each subsequent edition will be computed separately from the number of copies sold of prior editions.

7

**12. AUTHOR'S COPIES**

*Author can buy his own book from the publisher at a 50% discount.*

Publisher shall furnish to Author, free of charge, fifteen (15) copies and to the Agent, 5 free copies of the initial edition of the Work, and should Author desire more copies for personal use, Publisher shall supply such copies at one-half (1/2) the suggested retail price. No royalties shall be paid on copies purchased by Author. Author will be billed for such copies and payment shall be made within thirty (30) days of receipt of bill.

**13. AUTHOR'S MATERIALS**

*Important to those who sell or give away their books*

Publisher shall be responsible for only the same care of any of Author's materials in its custody as it takes of its own. However, except in the case of Publisher's gross negligence, Publisher shall not be responsible for loss or damage to any materials furnished by Author while in Publisher's custody or in the custody of anyone to whom delivery of such materials is necessary in connection with the production of the Work or is otherwise made with Author's consent. Author shall retain copies of any such materials and, in the case of photographs, the negative or duplicate positive of each photo furnished.

**14. EXCESS INVENTORY**

**a)** If at any time after one (1) year from publication of the work, Publisher has copies on hand which' in its judgement, cannot be sold through usual marketing channels. Publisher may sell such copies at a "Remainder Price". That is, at a special discount of sixty percent (60%) or more from the retail list or freight pass-through price. All copies sold at a Remainder Price shall be accounted for separately and not included in sales totals, and the royalty on each copy sold shall be ten percent (10%) of the net amount received by Publisher reduced by the manufacturing cost. Publisher will not pay any royalties on copies sold at or below manufacturing cost.

**b)** If the sale at a Remainder Price involves the entire inventory, Publisher will notify Author in advance of the planned sale and provide Author the opportunity to purchase all or part of the inventory at the manufacturing cost. Author must notify Publisher within thirty (30) days of the date of Publisher's notification as to whether or not Author wishes to make such purchase.

**15. WARRANTY AND INDEMNITY**

*This is important – if the book goes out of print, you want to be able to buy the remaining copies at a low price.*

**a) Warranty**

Author warrants and represents that:

**(i)** Author is the sole author and proprietor of the Work.

**(ii)** Author has full power and authority to make and perform this Agreement and to grant the rights granted hereunder, and Author has not previously assigned, transferred or otherwise encumbered the sale.

**(iii)** The Work is not in the public domain and has not previously been published, in the exclusive territory herein granted.

**(iv)** The Work does not infringe upon any statutory or common law copyright, or any trademark or service mark, or any literary property right.

**(v)** The Work does not invade the right of privacy or publicity of any person, nor contain any matter libelous or otherwise in contravention of the rights of any third party; and, if the Work is not a work of fiction, all statements in the Work asserted as facts are true and accurate.

**(vi)** The Work contains no matter which violates any federal or state statute or regulation thereunder, nor is it in any other manner unlawful.

**(vii)** The Work contains no recipe, formula or instruction which if reasonably followed would be injurious to the user.

**b)    Indemnity**
Author hereby indemnifies and agrees to hold Publisher, and seller of the Work and Publisher's licensees harmless from any claims, suits, action, losses, or damages, including reasonable attorneys' fees and disbursements, incurred or sustained by any of them, in connection with or resulting from any claim, suit, action, or proceeding arising out of, or relating to, a breach of any of Author's warranties, representations or agreements herein contained. In defending any such claim, action or proceeding, Publisher may use counsel of its own selection. Publisher shall promptly notify Author of any such claim, action, or proceeding. Publisher shall have the right to withhold its reasonable estimate of the total damages and expenses from sums otherwise payable to Author pursuant to this Agreement or any other agreement between Author and Publisher and to apply such sums to payment of such estimated damages and expenses. Any settlement of a claim, suit, action, or proceeding in excess of Five Thousand Dollars ($5,000) shall be subject to Author's approval, such approval not to be unreasonably withheld or delayed. In the event such claim, suit, action, or proceeding is discontinued or dismissed without liability to Publisher, Author shall be liable for and shall pay to Publisher fifty percent (50%) of the amount of Publisher's counsel fees and other expenses. *Note how contracts favor the publisher - not much you or I can do about it.*

**c) Survival of Warranties and Indemnities**
Any warranties, representations, agreements or indemnities contained io this paragraph shall survive the termination of or any reversion of rights under this agreement.

**16. OUT OF PRINT**    *Also important - If your book goes out of print, all rights should revert to you.*

**a)** The Work shall be considered in print if it is on sale by Publisher in any edition or if it is subject to an outstanding license under this Agreement. If the Work is not in print, Author may request in writing that Publisher keep the Work in print. Publisher will have six (6) months in which to comply. If Publisher fails to comply, or does not wish to keep the Work in print either by Publisher or any Licensee, then at the end of such six-month period this Agreement shall terminate and all of the rights granted to Publisher shall revert to Author, upon and subject to the payment by Author to Publisher of any outstanding indebtedness.

**b)** An unearned advance for the Work shall not be deemed an indebtedness.

**c)** In the event of termination under this paragraph 16 Author shall have the right to purchase the film or plates, if available, of the Work at one-third (1/3) of the manufacturing cost, including composition, and any remaining copies or sheets of the Work at the manufacturing cost. If Author does not elect to make this purchase within thirty (30) days, then Publisher may dispose of such materials as it sees fit.

9

**17. Publisher's Trademarks**
Author acknowledges that Publisher has sole and exclusive ownership of the trademark, trade name, logo, imprints and any other identification now or hereafter used by Publisher. Nothing in this Agreement (including, but not limited to, the right of Author to purchase books and film on termination) shall permit Author to use Publisher's identification during the term of this Agreement or thereafter, without first obtaining Publisher's consent in writing.

~~**18. Option**~~
~~Author agrees to offer to Publisher Author's next work or proposal~~ therefore before submitting the same to any other publisher. For a period of thirty (30) days after Publisher's receipt of the proposal. Author shall negotiate exclusively with Publisher. If at the end of such period, the parties are unable in good faith to reach a mutually satisfactory agreement, then Author may submit the proposal elsewhere; provided, however, that (i) Author shall not enter into a contract for publication of the work proposed upon terms less favorable to Author than those offered by Publisher, (ii) Author shall provide Publisher with the details of any terms offered prior to entering into any agreement with another publisher and (iii) Publisher shall have the right to acquire rights in the work proposed by matching all the material terms in the work proposed by matching all the material terms of the best bona fide offer for the work that the Author receives ~~from another publisher.~~

**19. Additional Documents**

**a)** Each party agrees to execute such documents as may be reasonably necessary to confirm the rights of the other party in respect to the Work.

**b)** If the Work has been previously published and the rights have reverted to Author, Author shall provide Publisher with the documentation relating to the reversion of the rights and certified copies of the original copyright registration certificate.

**20. Force Majeure**

Neither Author nor Publisher shall be liable because of delays in its performance caused by wars, civil riots, strikes, fires, acts of God, governmental restrictions or because of other similar circumstances beyond either party's control, provided such delay does not exceed three (3) months. If a party's performance is delayed for a period in excess of three (3) months, then the other party shall have the right to terminate this Agreement.

**21. Other Publications or Licenses**

**a)** Should an English-language foreign edition or other foreign-language edition of the Work be published prior to publication of the American edition, Author agrees to supply Publisher with one (1) copy of the first printing of the foreign edition, as soon as it is available, together with the exact date of publication of the foreign edition, so that Publisher may be assured that the American edition is protected according to the requirements of the American copyright law. The above copy and information will be sent to Contracts Director, Henry Holt and Company, Inc., 115 West 18th Street, New York, NY 10011.

10

**b)** In the event that foreign licensing rights and/or first serial rights are retained by Author, Author agrees to notify Publisher promptly of any arrangement made for publication of the Work in whole or in part in any language  including English, which would precede book publication in the United States. Author further agrees to consult with Publisher before licensing first serial rights.

**c)** During the term of this Agreement, Author agrees not to publish or authorize publication of any other work covering substantially the same subject matter as the Work which would be directly competitive to the work and likely to detract from, impair or frustrate Publisher's sales of the Work or Publisher's ability to exercise in full its rights in and to the Work.

22. **Agent**     *If this clause is not in the publisher's contract, your agent (if you use one) will add it.*

All sums due under this Agreement shall be paid and all statements, notices and communications hereunder shall be sent to:

__**Dominick Abel Literary Agency, Inc.     146 West 82nd Street**__

_____**New York, N.Y. 10024**_____(the "Agent"), which shall be a full and valid discharge of Publisher's obligations to Author with respect thereto, Publisher may rely on Agreement with respect to all matters under this Agreement, including settlement of any controversies arising under this agreement, unless Publisher has been previously notified in writing of termination of such agency.

Agent's Federal I.D. Number: __13-2990119__

**23. Miscellaneous Provisions**

**a)** This Agreement constitutes the complete understanding of the parties. No modification, waiver, or extension of any provision hereof shall be valid unless in writing and signed by both parties and no waiver shall be deemed a continuing one.

**b)** This Agreement shall be binding upon and shall inure to the benefit of the heirs and personal representatives of Author and the successors and assigns of Publisher. Author shall not assign his rights under this Agreement without the prior written consent of Publisher, except that without such consent Author may assign any net sums due him hereunder. Publisher may assign any right hereby granted to it, but may not, without the prior written consent of Author, assign this Agreement as an entirety except to a parent affiliate' or wholly owned subsidiary or in connection with the sale or transfer of substantially all its business or any division or department thereof.

**c)** Paragraph headings and captions have been inserted as a matter of convenience and do not define, alter, vary or serve to interpret any provision of this Agreement.

d) If there are multiple authors under this Agreement, the obligations of all the authors will be joint and several unless otherwise expressly provided in this Agreement, and Publisher may exercise any or ail of its remedies with respect to the authors individually or collectively. For the purposes of this agreement, all authors are to be collectively referred to as "Author".

11

**e)** This Agreement shall be deemed to have been entered into in the State of New York and shall be interpreted and construed in accordance with the laws if the State of New York applicable to agreements executed and to be performed therein by each party. Each party hereby agrees to submit to the sole and exclusive in personal jurisdiction of the courts of the State of New fork, New York County, for the resolution of all disputes between them or, if jurisdictional prerequisites exist at the time, to the sole and exclusive in personal jurisdiction of the Federal Courts of New York, with venue to be in the Southern District of New York.

**24.** The Author hereby irrevocably and in perpetuity appoints Dominick Abel Literary Agency, Inc. as his sole and exclusive Agent with respect to the Work and authorizes and directs the Publisher to make all payments due and/or to become due hereunder to the Author to and in the name of the said agent as a good and valid discharge of all such indebtedness. As the sole and exclusive agent, the said agent is hereby empowered by the Author to act in his behalf in all matters arising from and pertaining to this Agreement and to negotiate on behalf of the Author throughout the World as to the disposal of all rights reserved to the Author herein. For services rendered and to be rendered, the Author does hereby irrevocably and in perpetuity assign and transfer to the said agent, and the said agent is entitled to receive and retain, as his commission, as an agency coupled with an interest, a sum equal to ten percent (10%) of the gross monies accruing to the account of the Author hereunder, before any deductions from and charges against such monies for any reason whatsoever are made. The provisions of this paragraph shall survive the expiration and or termination of this Agreement.

**25.** Notwithstanding paragraphs 1, 4(c), and 4(d) the Author retains the right to sell copies of his work outside normal channels of trade distribution, and specifically, though not exclusively, by direct mail.

**26.** The Publisher agrees to permit the Author or his designated representative the right to inspect his books of account as related to the calculation and payment of royalties provided that such inspection shall be made during normal business hours and with reasonable cause. The Author or his designated representative shall provide to the Publisher in writing the basis for such reasonable cause at least 48 hours prior to such inspection. If errors of accounting amounting to five percent (5%) or more of the total sum paid to the Author shall be found to his disadvantage, the Publisher shall pay the sum owed to the Author within thirty (30) days plus eight percent (8%) interest; if the error is less than the said five percent (5%), the Publisher shall pay the sum due.

Author _____     Henry Holt and Company, Inc. _____

_____     By: _____

_____

Social Security No. (or Tax I.D. No.) _____

Citizenship _____

## *Schedule of Territories*

Agreement for:  ___Selling Your Services_____
Author:  ___Robert W. Bly_____
Publisher:  ___Henry Holt and Company, Inc._____

**Exclusive**
Countries marked x are licensed exclusively to Publisher.

**Reserved**
Countries marked x are reserved exclusively to Author.

Countries not marked or not appearing on this schedule are licensed nonexclusively to Publisher.

| Exclusive Reserved | Exclusive Reserved | Exclusive |
|---|---|---|

__ Indonesia ................ __

### SOUTH AMERICA

__ Argentina ............. __
__ Bolivia .................... __
__ Brazil ...................... __
__ Chile ...................... __
__ Colombia ................ __
__ Ecuador ................. __
__ Falkland Isl ............. x
__ Guiana (French) ......... __
__ Guyana .................... __
__ Paraguay ................. __
__ Peru ....................... __
__ Surinam .................. __
__ Uruguay .................. __
__ Venezuela ................ __

### ASIA

__ Afghanistan ............. __
__ Bahrain .................... x
__ Bangladesh .............. x
__ Bhutan .................... x
__ Brunei ..................... x
__ Burma ..................... x
__ Cambodia ................ x
__ China ...................... __
__ Hong Kong .............. x
__ India ....................... x

### ASIA *(con't)*

__ Iran ........................ __
__ Iraq ........................ __
__ Israel ...................... __
__ Japan ..................... __
__ Jordan .................... x
__ Korea ...................... __
__ Korea North ............ __
__ Kuwait .................... x
__ Laos ....................... __
__ Lebanon .................. __
__ Macao ..................... __
__ Malaysia .................. x
__ Maldives ................. __
__ Mongolia ................. __
__ Nepal ...................... x
__ Oman ...................... __
__ Pakistan .................. x
__ Philippines .............. __
__ Qatar ...................... __
__ Saudi Arabia ............ __
__ Singapore ................ x
__ Sri Lanka ................. __
__ Syria ....................... __
__ Taiwan .................... __
__ Thailand .................. __
__ Taiwan .................... __
__ Thailand .................. __
__ Turkey .................... __
__ United Arab Emirates. __
__ U.S.S.R. .................. __
__ Vietnam .................. __
__ Yemen .................... __
__ South Yemen ........... x

### EUROPE

__ Albania ................... __
__ Andorra ................... __
__ Austria .................... __
__ Belgium .................. __
__ Bulgaria .................. __
__ Cyprus .................... x
__ Czechoslovakia ........ __
__ Denmark ................. __
__ Finland ................... __
__ France .................... __
__ Germany, East ......... __
__ Germany, West ........ __
__ Gibraltar ................. x
__ Greece .................... __
__ Hungary .................. __
__ Iceland ................... __
__ Irish Republic ......... x
__ Italy ....................... __
__ Liechtenstein ........... __
__ Luxembourg ............ __
__ Malta ...................... x
__ Monaco ................... __
__ Netherlands ............ __
__ Norway ................... __
__ Poland .................... __
__ Portugal .................. __
__ Romania .................. __
__ San Marino ............. __
__ Spain ...................... __
__ Sweden ................... __
__ Switzerland ............. __

Initialized:  Author____
Publisher____

*We sold a Spanish edition for an advance of about $1,000*

# APPENDIX F

# SAMPLE PRESS RELEASE

When your book is published, the publisher will send the media a press release to publicize it. Most publishers have publicity departments that handle the writing and distribution of press releases; some may ask you to write it for them.

Magazine and newspaper editors as well as TV and radio program directors are constantly looking for news stories that will be of interest to their audience. To be effective, the press release should present an interesting story in a concise manner with all the relevant information laid out clearly. Contact information is included to allow the editor or program director to request additional information and a review copy of the book.

Here is the press release for *How To Get Your Book Published.* In addition to highlighting the new and unique features of the book and how they benefit the reader, the press release also adds a human interest angle by including quotes from the author.

# PRESS RELEASE

For Immediate Release
For more information contact:
Robert Kalian    (1-888) 229-3733

## NEW BOOK SHOWS WRITERS HOW TO GET THEIR BOOK PUBLISHED

Robert W. Bly, one of America's most prolific non-fiction book authors has now written a guide that aspiring writers everywhere will find invaluable.

*How To Get Your Book Published - Inside Secrets of A Successful Author* is a highly informative step-by-step guide that draws entirely on Bly's experiences in getting an incredible 45 books published in the last 16 years, with 10 more under contract.

Bly's recent titles include *The Elements of Business Writing* (Macmillan), *How To Sell Your House, Coop, or Condo* (Consumer Report Books), *Secrets of a Freelance Writer* (Holt), and *Keeping Your Clients Satisfied* (Prentice Hall).

"I believe that everyone has a book inside them and can write their book and sell it to a publisher by following my proven eight-step method," says Bly a New Milford, NJ resident who at age 39 has seen his books published by a half dozen of the biggest publishing firms in the country.

"It's not lack of book ideas or writing ability that prevents writers from getting their book published. And it's not lack of determination. Rather it's lack of knowledge of just how the publishing industry works. The difference between published authors and aspiring writers is that successful authors have learned how to package and sell their book ideas to publishers. That's exactly the information I reveal in *How To Get Your Book Published*."

According to Bly, one of the biggest mistakes a new author can make is to write the book before finding a publisher for it. "They spend months researching and writing a book only to find that editors want to see book proposals not a finished book," says Bly. "Editors don't have the time to read unsolicited manuscripts. They prefer to get a brief outline of the book you propose to write. In fact, submitting the completed book marks you as an amateur and actually diminishes your chances for a sale," Bly insists.

Another common mistake novices make is to propose books that interest them personally but have no appeal to the book-buying public. "The book has to tell an interesting story, provide useful advice, or contain valuable reference information the reader cannot get elsewhere," says Bly. "Be sure you can answer the question 'Why would someone spend $14.95 for this book and spend hours reading it instead of watching TV?'"

*How To Get Your Book Published* covers all of the steps needed to research, write and sell your book to a publisher including: developing a saleable book idea, evaluating the market, writing a powerful book proposal, getting a literary agent to represent you, negotiating your advance and royalties, and selling the book to a publisher. Designed as a practical hands-on guide, the book includes actual book proposals and one of Bly's book contracts annotated with his commentary plus directories of major publishers, literary agents, ghostwriters and more.

*How To Get Your Book Published* is available in stores nationwide. It can also be ordered directly from the publisher by sending $14.95 plus $3.00 s&h to: Roblin Press, 405 Tarrytown Road  PMB 414-GBP, White Plains, NY 10607 (To order by phone call: 1-914-347-5934). It is sold with a 30 day money-back guarantee.

To arrange for an interview with the author or for a review copy of the book, editors may call Linda Kalian at 1-888-229-3733.

# APPENDIX G

# SAMPLE AUTHOR'S QUESTIONNAIRE

At some point prior to publication of your book, your publisher will ask you to complete and return an *Author's Questionnaire*, similar to the one shown below. Although it requires a lot of information, take the time to complete the form as accurately and fully as possible. The better your answers, the better the publisher can promote your book. Take a look at this sample questionnaire and, if you are working on a book, start gathering the information to complete your questionnaire now.

---

## AUTHOR QUESTIONNAIRE

Working Title: _____

Author (as you want it to appear on your book): _____

_____

Co-author(s): _____

Home Address: _____

    Phone & Fax: _____

Business address: _____

    Phone & Fax: _____

Date and place of birth: _____

Present occupation: _____

Previous occupations: _____

_____

Professional affiliations that might have a bearing on the marketing of your book: _____

_____

_____

AUTHOR QUESTIONNAIRE      -2-

Local newspaper (include complete address): _____

_____

_____

Provide a short biographical sketch which might be useful in the promotion of your book: _____

_____

_____

_____

_____

Please give full titles, publication dates and publishers of any previously published works: _____

_____

_____

_____

Please write 75 to 100 words on the book's theme, intent and underlying concept: _____

_____

_____

_____

_____

_____

_____

What is the audience for your book? Name the specific ways it benefits the reader. What is unique about it? _____

_____

_____

_____

_____

Would the potential buyer of your book belong to a specific profession? Any society or organization? Any ethnic group? List any special interest groups where there might be particular interest: _____

_____

_____

_____

AUTHOR QUESTIONNAIRE                                    -3-

Do you have any personal contacts at magazines, film companies or book clubs who might assist us in exploring subsidiary rights of your book? Please give full names, titles and address: _____

_____

_____

_____

_____

Are there any reviewers, columnists or other media people who might `be particularly receptive to your book and might give it media attention? _

_____

_____

_____

_____

What publications should be considered as advertising media to reach the most interested readers for your book?_____

_____

_____

_____

Please list any previous radio or television appearances: _____

_____

_____

_____

List any bookshops in your neighborhood that might give your book special display, etc. If possible, include the name of the manager:_____

_____

_____

_____

Will you be attenting any conferences in the coming year at which it might be appropriate to display and/or offer for sale copies of your book? Please list them together with dates: _____

_____

_____

_____

_____

AUTHOR QUESTIONNAIRE                                                    -4-

List any cities or areas where there might be special interest in your book:

_____

_____

_____

_____

_____

List any companies or stores which might be interested in a bulk purchase of your book:

_____

_____

_____

Are mailing lists available of the key people who would buy your book: Where can these lists be obtained? _____

_____

_____

_____

_____

Are there any special interest magazines, journals or associations that may want to sell your book to their readers or members? Please provide complete addresses: _____

_____

_____

_____

_____

Please suggest any special non-bookstore markets or ideas that we might consider to help the sale of your book? _____

_____

_____

_____

_____

Thank you for your time and effort!

# APPENDIX H

# SELECTED PUBLICATIONS
# FOR WRITERS

*Canadian Writer's Journal*
PO Box 6618, Depot 1
Victoria, BC
V8P 5N7 Canada

*Children's Book Insider*
P.O. Box 1030
Fairplay, CO 80440-1030
800-807-1916 or (719) 836-0394

*New Writer's Magazine*
Sarasota Bay Publishing
PO Box 5976
Sarasota, FL 34277-5976
(813) 953-7903

*The New York Times Book Review*
229 W. 43rd Street
New York, NY 10036
(212) 556-1234

*Poet's And Writer's*
72 Spring Street
New York, NY 10012
(212) 226-3586

*Publishers' Weekly*
249 W. 17th Street
New York, NY 10011
(800) 278-2991

*The Writer*
120 Boylston Street
Boston, MA 02116
(617) 423-3157

*Writer's Digest*
1507 Dana Avenue
Cincinnati, Ohio 45207
(513) 531-2690

# APPENDIX I

# SELECTED ORGANIZATIONS FOR WRITERS

Here are some writer's clubs and organizations you may want to join. These are useful for getting leads to agents, editors, and publishers, as well as for learning more about the business and craft of writing by talking with your fellow writers — both those at your level as well as those who have been more widely published.

American Medical Writers Association
160 Fifth Avenue, Suite 625
New York, NY 10010
(212) 645-2368

American Society for Journalists and Authors
1501 Broadway, Suite 302
New York, NY 10036
(212) 997-0947

The Author's Guild
330 W. 42nd Street, 29th floor
New York, NY 10036
(212) 563-5904

The Author's League of America
330 West 42nd St  29th Floor
New York, NY 10036-6902
(212) 564-8350

Education Writers Association
1331 H. NW, Suite 307
Washington, DC 20036
(202) 637-9700

Cassell Network of Writers/
Florida Freelance Writers Association
PO Box A
North Stratford, NH 03590
(800) 351-9278

National Association of Science Writers
Box 294
Greenlawn, NY 11740
(516) 757-5664

National Writer's Union
873 Broadway, Suite 203
New York, NY 10003
(212) 254-0279

Outdoor Writers Association of America, Inc.
2017 Cato Avenue, Suite 101
State College, PA 16801-2768

SWAN
Self Employed Artist's and Writer's Network
(201) 967-1313

Society of American Travel Writers
4101 Lake Boone Trail, Suite 201
Raleigh, NC 27607
(919) 787-5181

Society of Children's Book Writers and Illustrators
22736 Vanowen St., Suite 106
West Hills, CA 91307
(818) 888-8760

Western Writers of America, Inc.
416 Bedford Road
El Paso, TX 79922-1204

# APPENDIX J

# A GLOSSARY OF BOOK PUBLISHING TERMS

**Acquisitions editor:** Editor at a publishing house responsible for acquiring new titles and negotiating book contracts with agents and authors.

**Advance:** Up-front money paid to the author against his or her future royalties.

**Auction:** An agent submits a book manuscript, proposal, or idea to several publishers who are interested in it, and they bid against one another for the right to publish it.

**Backlist:** Older books that have the potential to remain in print and continue to sell a respectable amount of copies (say, 2,000 or more per year) over an extended period of time.

**Back matter:** Material that appears in the back of a book, after the main text. Includes appendices, the index, and author's biography.

**Best seller:** Any book that makes it onto the best-seller lists of one or more of the nation's major daily newspapers.

**Blurb:** A favorable comment about the book, reprinted on the book's cover, inside pages, or advertisements for the book.

**Bound galleys:** A small quantity of galleys are cut into page proofs that are bound, like a book, only with a cover of plain cardboard or heavy paper stock instead of glossy paper or cloth.

**Copyedited manuscript:** The author's manuscript marked

with suggested edits made by the copy editor, and submitted to the author for both approval and revision purposes.

**Electronic rights:**  Offering, with permission, all or part of a book's contents through electronic media such as the Internet, disks, or CD-ROMs.

**Exclusive submission:**  Submitting a book proposal, idea, or manuscript to one publisher and given them the opportunity to make an offer on it, without competition, for a limited period of time.

**First serial:**  Reprinting, with permission, a portion of the book in a magazine or other printed medium before the book is published.

**Frontlist:**  New or recently updated books.

**Front matter:**  Material in the front of the book that comes before the main text. Includes the title page, dedication, acknowledgments, preface, introduction, copyright page, and table of contents.

**Galleys:**  Long proof sheets of the book manuscript set in type, provided to the author for proofreading purposes.

**Gross royalty:**  A royalty based on a percentage of the cover price of the book.

**Hard cover:**  A book with a hard cover.

**Internet Publishing:**  Posting your manuscript as a downloadable file on the Internet where is may be bought and downloaded as an electronic file.

**ISBN (International Standard Book Number):**  A number that identifies the title and the publisher of a book. Every book has its own individual ISBN.

**Literary agent:** A professional who acts as an author's representative, selling their writings to publishers, usually in exchange for a percentage of the advances and royalties paid.

**Mainstream publisher:** One of the top 100 or so large, well-known publishing houses, perhaps the best known of which to the general public is Doubleday.

**Mass market paperback:** A small paperback designed to be easily carried by the reader. Sold in bookstores, drug stores, and supermarkets.

**Net royalty:** A royalty based on the amount of money the publisher actually receives for the book. If a book costs $10 and the bookstore pays $6 for it, the net royalty is a percentage of $6, not $10.

**Page proofs:** Checking copies of the book in its final page layout prior to printing. Page proofs are essentially galleys cut and divided into individual pages and numbered in order.

**Print-On-Demand Publishing:** The ability brought about by modern computer technology to print individual copies of a book as they are needed.

**Publication date ('Pub date'):** The official date of publication for a book. Usually this date is set as three to four months later than the actual date the book is printed. This is done to allow the media to review the book prior to the official publication date.

**Publisher**: Any individual or organization that publishes written materials such as books, newsletters, and magazines.

**Publishing house:** Another term for a publishing company.

**Query letter:** The letter you send to an agent or publisher to see if they'd be interested in looking at your book proposal or manuscript (see Chapter 7 for a sample query letter).

**Remainder:** Copies of out of print books the publisher no longer wants. Remainders can be sold to the author, a specialty remainder distributor, or used as landfill.

**Royalty:** A fee paid to an author based on the number of books sold, and calculated as a percentage of the book's price.

**Returns:** Copies of books ordered by bookstores and then returned to the publisher because the stores did not sell them. Authors do not earn royalties on returns.

**SASE:** Self-addressed stamped envelope. Include a SASE whenever you send a query letter or book proposal to an agent or publisher.

**Second serial:** Publication of a portion of your book in a magazine or other print medium, with permission, after the book is published.

**Self-publishing:** Typesetting, printing, distributing and marketing your book on your own.

**Simultaneous submission:** Submitting your proposal or manuscript to more than one publisher at a time. Perfectly acceptable in today's market, as long as you don't lie about it.

**Trade paperback:** A full-size paperback that is, essentially, identical to a hardcover except that the cover is paper, not cloth.

**Traditional publishing:** Getting your book in print by selling it to a mainstream publisher.

**Trim size:** The length and width dimensions of the finished book's pages and covers.

**University press:** A publishing house that is affiliated with a university.

**Vanity press:** A publisher that charges the author an up-front fee to print and publish his/her book.

# APPENDIX K

# BOOK DOCTORS, EDITORS, GHOSTWRITERS, AND OTHERS WHO CAN HELP PUT YOUR MANUSCRIPT INTO SHAPE

Author's, Publishers, and Writer's Hotline
7 Putter Lane
Middle Island, NY
516-924-8555

American Society of Journalists and Authors
New York, NY
(212) 997-0947

David Kohn
3117 Lake Shore Drive
Deerfield Beach, FL 33442
954-429-9373

Editorial Freelancers Association
New York, NY
(212) 929-5400

Jerry Gross
63 Grand Street
Croton on Hudson, NY 10520-2518
(914) 271-8704

Scott Michel Literary Services
80 Broome Avenue
Atlantic Beach, NY 11506
(516) 239-7092

Toby Stein
45 Church Street
Montclair, NJ 07042
(201) 744-0475

Joe Vitale
303 Mill Stream Lane
Houston, TX 77060
713-999-1110

William Greenleaf
525 E. Stonebridge Drive
Gilbert, AZ 85234

New York Editors
521 Fifth Avenue  17th Floor
New York, NY 10175

Free Expressions
3780 W. Lucas Suite 239
Beaumont, TX 77706
(409) 892-3522

Zebra Communications
Suite 203  #255
4651 Woodstock Road
Roswell, GA 30075

Gary Robert Muschia
Box 172
South River, NJ 08882
(908) 390-0683

Irene Frankel
P.O. Box 2075
Hoboken, NJ 07030
(201) 798-0298

# ABOUT THE AUTHOR

Bob Bly has been a professional writer since 1979 and a full-time freelance writer since 1982.

Bob is the author of more than 100 articles and 45 books including *Creative Careers: Real Jobs in Glamour Fields* (John Wiley & Sons), *The Elements of Business Writing* (Macmillan), *The Elements of Technical Writing* (Macmillan), *The Copywriter's Handbook* (Henry Holt & Co.), and *Secrets of a Freelance Writer* (Henry Holt & Co.). His success rate in selling books to publishers is over 90 percent.

Bob's latest book is *Careers for Writers*, published by VGM Career Horizons. Other titles include The *Ultimate Unauthorized Star Trek Quiz Book* (HarperCollins), *Comic Book Heroes* (Carol Publishing), *Why You Should Never Beam Down in a Red Shirt* (HarperCollins), *How to Sell Your House, Co-op or Condo* (Consumer Reports Books), *Power-Packed Direct Mail* (Henry Holt & Co.), *Keeping Clients Satisfied* (Prentice Hall), and *The "I Hate Kathie Lee Gifford" Book* (Kensington).

Mr. Bly's articles have appeared in such publications as *Amtrak Express, Computer Decisions, Cosmopolitan, City Paper, Science Books & Films, The Money Paper, New Jersey Monthly,* and *Writer's Digest.* Bob has been a featured speaker at writers' conferences nationwide. Thousands of writers have attended in person or listened to on tape his popular seminars, "How to Write a Nonfiction Book and Get It Published" and "How to Make $85,000+ a Year as a Freelance Writer."

Mr. Bly has held a number of writing-related jobs. He was a technical writer for Westinghouse Electric Corporation and an advertising manager for Koch Engineering. As a freelance copywriter, he has handled writing assignments for dozens of corporations including AT&T, IBM, ITT, Value Line, Medical Economics, Reed Travel Group, Plato Software, Hyperion Software, Wallace & Tiernan, BOC Gases, Computron, Leviton Manufacturing, Associated Air Freight, Agora Publishing, Phillips Publishing, Timeplex, McGraw-Hill, and Chemical Bank.

Questions and comments on *How To Get Your Book Published* may be sent to:  Bob Bly
22 E. Quackenbush Avenue
Dumont, NJ 07628
Phone (201) 385-1220
fax (201) 385-1138
e-mail: Rwbly@bly.com

# Index